OBAMA

The HISTORIC PRESIDENCY

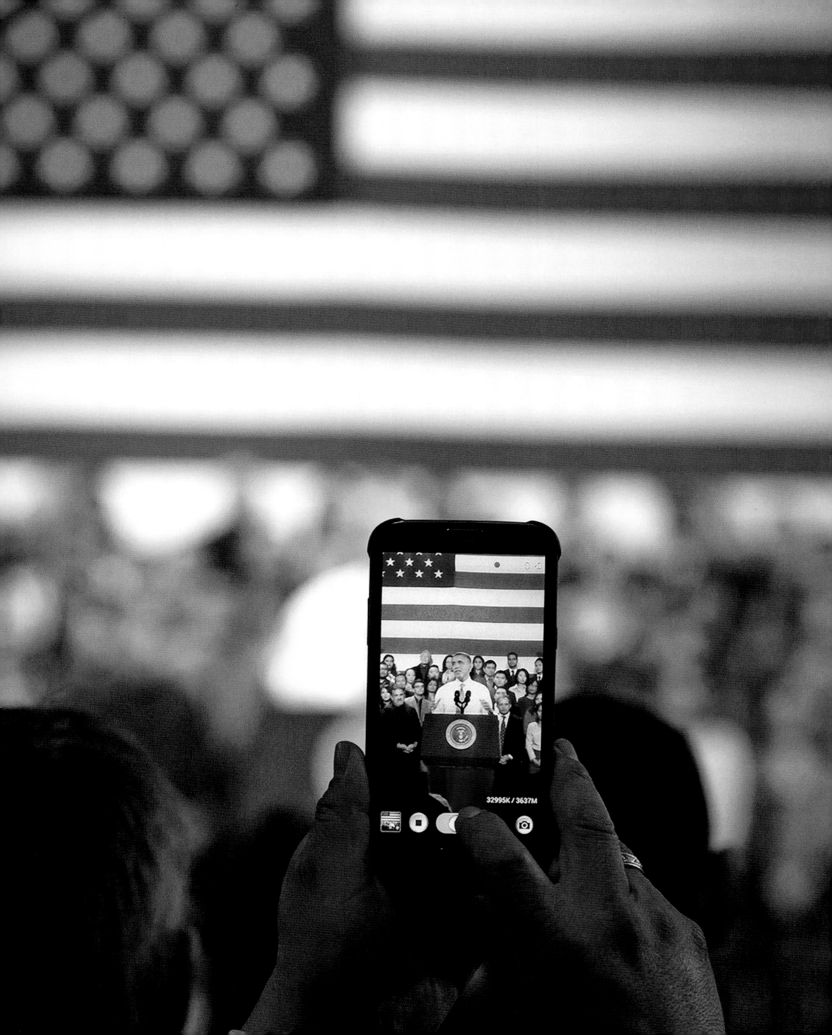

OBAMA

The HISTORIC PRESIDENCY *of* BARACK OBAMA | *2,920 Days*

Created by MARK GREENBERG | *Foreword by* KEN BURNS

Written by DAVID TAIT, OBE

with MARK GREENBERG *and* BARBARA BALCH

STERLING
New York

STERLING
New York

An Imprint of Sterling Publishing Co., Inc.
1166 Avenue of the Americas
New York, NY 10036

ISBN 978-1-4549-2639-9

Distributed in Canada by Sterling Publishing Co., Inc.
c/o Canadian Manda Group, 664 Annette Street
Toronto, Ontario, Canada M6S 2C8
Distributed in the United Kingdom by GMC Distribution Services
Castle Place, 166 High Street, Lewes, East Sussex, England BN7 1XU
Distributed in Australia by NewSouth Books
45 Beach Street, Coogee, NSW 2034, Australia

For information about custom editions, special sales, and premium
and corporate purchases, please contact Sterling Special Sales at
800-805-5489 or specialsales@sterlingpublishing.com.

Manufactured in Canada

2 4 6 8 10 9 7 5 3 1

www.sterlingpublishing.com

Interior design by Barbara Balch

Photo Credits see page 207

CONTENTS

BARACK HUSSEIN OBAMA takes the oath of office, January 20, 2009.

HISTORY WILL BE very kind to Barack Obama. His administration will go down as one of the most consequential in all of American history: its achievements—often overlooked or reflexively rejected—are among the three or four most transformative presidencies in the last turbulent century; his personal conduct, discipline, and rectitude reminiscent of the Founding Fathers; his oratorical gifts and passionate empathy unequalled in American letters; his breakthrough election a watershed moment as the nation tried to escape the specific gravity of its troubled racial past.

"Black Man Given Nation's Worst Job," the *Onion* satirically joked after his election in November 2008. But in many ways it wasn't funny, rather terrifyingly prescient. It prefigured the retrograde forces that would relentlessly try to derail his progressive agenda from the moment he took the oath of office, suggesting to us now in retrospect that this malevolent counter-narrative of the Obama years must be given equal weight with the optimistic narrative he tried so heroically, and mostly successfully, to write.

Though many will try, the democratic energies he released—so hopeful, inclusive, fair, and muscular— will not be kidnapped and reconfined. The bells of hope he rang cannot be unrung. And though many will want to go backward, Americans will not accept anything less than universal healthcare, equal pay, marriage equality, wise environmental stewardship, infrastructure improvements, a robust economy combined with job creation, and a rational relationship to the world. He moved us forward—permanently— in so many ways big and small. And he did it all while remaining an extraordinary father and husband. This is his enduring legacy.

"Don't Do Stupid Stuff" was his mantra—and he didn't. Period. For eight complicated years there were no scandals or headline-grabbing investigations, only a thoughtful approach to every problem, every day. He was inspiring, confident, funny, loving, and so blessed with an appreciation of the American promise he had gracefully inherited that he paid it forward, helping to mint an entire generation of citizens dedicated to achieving positive change—activism within the system. All of it heralded a new persuasive expression of American *possibilities*.

He spoke to us with words so carefully crafted that comparisons to his hero, Abraham Lincoln, are not only appropriate but accurate. He cried with us when grief was our only outlet, sang with us in common sorrow, danced with us in collective joy, and made his administration look like the diverse country he was charged with representing. He was fearless but moderated, assiduously avoiding the foreign entanglements George Washington had warned us about, but when it mattered, did not hesitate to take out our most dangerous enemy. Like Lincoln, he understood how far we (and he) had come on our collective journey, but as our religious teachings constantly try to remind us, he also understood *in his bones* that the greatest enemy is often ourselves, our ancient animosities and stubborn prejudices so hard to shed.

The great early twentieth-century African American scholar W. E. B. Du Bois liked to challenge the "talented tenth"—better-off black Americans who would assume the difficult task of lifting the rest of the race upward. That, of course, would require enormous sacrifice, and focus, and dedication. Ten decades later, Barack Obama, along with his remarkable wife, Michelle, had to work ten times as hard as that to do the job. But he has shown us all—black, white, brown, *every one* of us—what a "talented 1 percent" might look like. We are all the beneficiaries of his exquisite example. He will be missed.

—Ken Burns
Walpole, New Hampshire
January 26, 2017

"IN MY LIFETIME" is a curious expression, as we never really know how long our lifetime will be.

In the thick of the 2008 primary season, I had an interesting question posed to me by the head of the Hackensack University Medical Center's Organ Transplatation Division: "Do you want to know how much longer you have to live?" Just like that. His demeanor was strictly matter of fact, his eyes glancing about his desk, and then, after a millisecond's pregnant pause, he added, "If we don't find you a suitable blood marrow donor."

My first reaction probably should have been to think how dreadful it was for a doctor to throw compassion to the wind in such a way with a patient whose life might soon be cut short. Instead, however, I almost laughed out loud at his clearly well-practiced disconnect. And then my mind started fast-forwarding to all the things I may never see, know, or experience: my daughters marrying and becoming mothers, me becoming a grandfather. Would I ever make it to Dollywood? Next, the political junkie in me kicked in: Would I live to see the first African American president or first female president?

I got lucky; in April 2008, a "suitable" donor was found. A complete stranger was identified as the proverbial "10," which in this case meant we had 10 out of 10 matching genetic markers. A month later, one of my two transplant doctors opened the valve on the bag containing the donor's life-sustaining marrow, which would give me the chance of a few more years.

I liked both of the Democratic candidates, and as I lay in my hospital bed over the next three weeks, I probably spent way too much energy worrying that neither of them might make it to the Promised Land. How wonderful the thought, however, that finally that iconic, poster-like image of the past 43 presidents— all white, all male—might soon have an incongruous face. And it was about time. Would I live to see the first woman or first African American president in my lifetime? Well, I am writing this, am I not?

For all modern presidents, the markers seem to have become the now infamous "On day one I'm going to . . ." and the judgment offered up by the media of the first hundred days. In my case, if I could survive the first 100 days out of transplant, there was a 2-to-1 chance I may survive the first year. And after that milestone, I might finally be designated a "survivor" and be released from the transplant unit's oversight. The team, my family, and my friends were pulling for me, praying for me, and displaying all their better selves to insure my return to health.

Unlike most presidents, Barack Obama seemed not to have the proper DNA to be afforded a good match with the bodies of Congress and their almost vicious "take no prisoners" approach to his presidency. He never had the traditional honeymoon of 100 days, and, in fact, the lead member of the attacking party stated on October 23, 2010, that "The single most important thing we want to achieve is for President Obama to be a one-term president." To be fair, in the context of the full interview, the statement was a summation of a balanced political conversation, but the point was clear; in order to make sure the president failed, the party had to line up in lockstep behind its leader.

As for me, I suffered through two years of a chronic rejection known medically as graft-versus-host disease. I was the host, and my unknown donor was the graft. For the next five years, I referred to him as "Spartacus," as, like the legendary gladiator, he had selflessly stood up to radically alter the outcome of an almost impossible situation.

Barack Obama suffered eight years of a similar condition of rejection and did so with unprecedented class, intellectual strength, limitless resolve, boundless wit, joy, and buckets of charm.

—Mark Greenberg

P.S. If you were wondering—as of now, I still haven't made it to Dollywood.

THE WEDNESDAY, November 5, 2008, front page of the *Anniston Star* of Alabama epitomizes the jubilant mood across the country, and the world, the day after Barack Obama was elected the 44th U.S. president.

PHOTOJOURNALIST Marc PoKempner followed a young Barack Obama while campaigning for the Illinois State Senate in 1995; here, PoKempner's photograph of Obama talking with a group of children on the South Shore of Chicago in 1995. At the time, PoKempner, like many of his peers, thought, "This man could be president one day."

PRESIDENT BARACK OBAMA posing
at the White House while digital imaging
experts from the Smithsonian Institute and
USC Institute for Creative Technologies scan
his face for digitally printed 3-D bust and life
mask portraits. June 2014.

"Hope is not blind optimism. It's not ignoring the enormity of the task ahead or the roadblocks that stand in our path. It's not sitting on the sidelines or shirking from a fight. Hope is that thing inside us that insists, despite all the evidence to the contrary, that something better awaits us if we have the courage to reach for it, and to work for it, and to fight for it. . . . [Hope is] the belief that destiny will not be written for us, but by us, by all those men and women who are not content to settle for the world as it is, who have the courage to remake the world as it should be."

—BARACK OBAMA, address to supporters
after the Iowa caucuses, January 3, 2008.

THE BEGINNING

Life has many beginnings—childhood, school, love, career—and all have their own starting points. For Barack Hussein Obama, the unlikely road to the Oval Office began in Hawaii, where his Kenyan father, also named Barack, was a foreign student. His mother, Mary, originally from Kansas, was white—she and his father had married when she was just eighteen. Mary's subsequent divorce and remarriage took young Barack to Indonesia for four years before returning to Hawaii, where his white grandparents raised him.

An outstanding student, Barack made it into Honolulu's highly regarded Punahou School. Then it was on to Columbia University in New York, graduating from there with a political science degree in 1983. Consumed with a desire to change the world, the twenty-two-year-old's next beginning took him to the impoverished South Side of Chicago, where he found work as a community organizer for a small faith-based group. It gave the young Ivy Leaguer an insight into the neighborhood's bleak inner city life that would stick with him forever. In 1988, Barack's further education began again at Harvard Law School, where in 1990 he became the first African American president of the prestigious *Harvard Law Review*. Leaving Harvard, the world was his oyster, but Barack's Chicago experiences had left an indelible impression. He headed back to the Windy City, where, eschewing offers from major law firms, he opted to practice civil rights law for a small public-interest firm.

Princeton graduate Michelle Robinson had also attended Harvard Law, earning her degree a year earlier than Barack. Their paths would not cross, however, until, while working at a Chicago law firm, she was asked to advise a summer associate with "an unusual name." Love led to still more beginnings—their 1992 marriage, Malia's birth in 1998, and Sasha's in 2001.

Obama's political career began in 1996 when he won a seat in the Illinois State Senate. But the "beginning of all beginnings" would come in 2004 when, while running for the U.S. Senate, he was invited to deliver the keynote address at the 2004 Democratic National Convention. With the memorable words—"There's not a liberal America and a conservative America—there's the United States of America," the beginning had begun. Four years later, he became the first African American to accept the Democrats' nomination for president. ★

Previous pages:
DELEGATES CHEER DURING the speech by keynote speaker Barack Obama, candidate for the U.S. Senate from Illinois, at the Democratic National Convention at the FleetCenter in Boston, July 27, 2004.

Opposite:
DEMOCRATIC PRESIDENTIAL NOMINEE Barack Obama arrives onstage for the Democratic National Convention at Invesco Field, Denver, Colorado, August 28, 2008—the first black major-party nominee.

VICTORY SPEECH

November 4, 2008 | GRANT PARK, CHICAGO, ILLINOIS

ELLO, CHICAGO. IF there is anyone out there who still doubts that America is a place where all things are possible; who still wonders if the dream of our founders is alive in our time; who still questions the power of our democracy, tonight is your answer.

It's the answer told by lines that stretched around schools and churches in numbers this nation has never seen; by people who waited three hours and four hours, many for the first time in their lives, because they believed that this time must be different; that their voices could be that difference.

It's the answer spoken by young and old, rich and poor, Democrat and Republican, black, white, Hispanic, Asian, Native American, gay, straight, disabled, and not disabled—Americans who sent a message to the world that we have never been just a collection of individuals or a collection of red states and blue states: we are, and always will be, the United States of America.

It's the answer that led those who have been told for so long by so many to be cynical, and fearful, and doubtful about what we can achieve—to put their hands on the arc of history and bend it once more toward the hope of a better day.

It's been a long time coming, but tonight, because of what we did on this day, in this election, at this defining moment, change has come to America.

A little bit earlier this evening, I received an extraordinarily gracious call from Senator McCain. Senator McCain fought long

WHO NEEDS CALIFORNIA? Even before California's 55 electoral votes were counted, CNN was calling an Obama victory.

and hard in this campaign, and he's fought even longer and harder for the country that he loves. He has endured sacrifices for America that most of us cannot begin to imagine, and we are better off for the service rendered by this brave and selfless leader. I congratulate him, I congratulate Governor Palin for all they have achieved, and I look forward to working with them to renew this nation's promise in the months ahead.

I want to thank my partner in this journey, a man who campaigned from his heart and spoke for the men and women he grew up with on the streets of Scranton and rode with on the train home to Delaware, the vice president-elect of the United States, Joe Biden.

And I would not be standing here tonight without the unyielding support of my best friend for the last sixteen years, the rock of our family and the love of my life, our nation's next first lady, Michelle Obama. Sasha and Malia, I love you both more than you can imagine, and you have earned the new puppy that's coming with us to the White House. And while she's no longer with us, I know my grandmother is watching, along with the family that made me who I am. I miss them tonight. I know that my debt to them is beyond measure. To my sister Maya, my sister Auma, all my other brothers and sisters, thank you so much for all the support that you've given me. I'm grateful to them.

To my campaign manager David Plouffe, the unsung hero of this campaign, who built the best political campaign, I think, in the history of the United States of America. To my chief strategist David Axelrod, who's been a partner with me every

A NEW FIRST family is born. Grant Park, Chicago, November 5, 2008.

step of the way. To the best campaign team ever assembled in the history of politics—you made this happen, and I am forever grateful for what you've sacrificed to get it done.

But above all, I will never forget who this victory truly belongs to—it belongs to you. It belongs to you.

I was never the likeliest candidate for this office. We didn't start with much money or many endorsements. Our campaign was not hatched in the halls of Washington—it began in the backyards of Des Moines and the living rooms of Concord and the front porches of Charleston.

It was built by working men and women who dug into what little savings they had to give five dollars and ten dollars and twenty dollars to the cause. It drew strength from the young people who rejected the myth of their generation's apathy; who left their homes and their families for jobs that offered little pay and less sleep; it drew strength from the not-so-young people who braved the bitter cold and scorching heat to knock on the doors of perfect strangers; and from the millions of Americans who volunteered, and organized, and proved that more than two centuries later, a government of the people, by the people, and for the people has not perished from the Earth. This is your victory. I know you didn't do this just to win an election, and I know you didn't do it for me. You did it because you understand the enormity of the task that lies ahead. For even as we celebrate tonight, we know the challenges that tomorrow will bring are the greatest of our lifetime—two wars, a planet in peril, the worst financial crisis in a century. Even as we stand here tonight, we know there are brave Americans waking up in the deserts of Iraq and the mountains of Afghanistan to risk their lives for us. There are mothers and fathers who will lie awake after their children fall asleep and wonder how they'll make the mortgage, or pay their doctor's bills, or save enough for their child's college education. There is new energy to harness, new jobs to be created, new schools to build, and threats to meet, [and] alliances to repair.

The road ahead will be long. Our climb will be steep. We may not get there in one year or even in one term, but, America—I have never been more hopeful than I am tonight that we will get there. I promise you—we as a people will get there.

There will be setbacks and false starts. There are many who won't agree with every decision or policy I make as president, and we know that government can't solve every problem. But I will always be honest with you about the challenges we face. I will listen to you, especially when we disagree. And above all, I will ask you to join in the work of remaking this nation the only way it's been done in America for 221 years—block by block, brick by brick, calloused hand by calloused hand.

What began 21 months ago in the depths of winter cannot end on this autumn night. This victory alone is not the change we seek—it is only the chance for us to make that change. And that cannot happen if we go back to the way things were. It can't happen without you, a new spirit of service, a new spirit of sacrifice.

So let us summon a new spirit of patriotism; of responsibility, where each of us resolves to pitch in and work harder and look after not only ourselves but each other.

"The road ahead will be long. Our climb will be steep. We may not get there in one year or even one term, but America—I have never been more hopeful than I am tonight that we will get there. I promise you—we as a people will get there."

Let us remember that if this financial crisis taught us anything, it's that we cannot have a thriving Wall Street while Main Street suffers—in this country, we rise or fall as one nation; as one people.

Let us resist the temptation to fall back on the same partisanship and pettiness and immaturity that has poisoned our politics for so long. Let us remember that it was a man from this state who first carried the banner of the Republican Party to the White House—a party founded on the values of self-reliance, individual liberty, and national unity. Those are values that we all share, and while the Democratic Party has won a great victory tonight, we do so with a measure of humility and determination to heal the divides that have held back our progress. As Lincoln said to a nation far more divided than ours, "We are not enemies but friends . . . though passion may have strained, it must not break our bonds of affection." And to those Americans whose support I have yet to earn—I may not have won your vote tonight, but I hear your voices, I need your help, and I will be your president, too.

And to all those watching tonight from beyond our shores, from parliaments and palaces to those who are huddled around radios in the forgotten corners of the world—our stories are singular, but our destiny is shared, and a new dawn of American leadership is at hand. To those who would tear the world down—we will defeat you. To those who seek peace and security—we support you. And to all those who have wondered if America's beacon still burns as bright—tonight we proved once more that the true strength of our nation comes not from our the might of our arms or the scale of our wealth but from the enduring power of our ideals: democracy, liberty, opportunity, and unyielding hope.

That's the true genius of America—that America can change. Our union can be perfected. And what we have already achieved gives us hope for what we can and must achieve tomorrow.

This election had many firsts and many stories that will be told for generations. But one that's on my mind tonight is about a woman who cast her ballot in Atlanta. She's a lot like the millions of others who stood in line to make their voice heard in this election except for one thing—Ann Nixon Cooper is 106 years old.

She was born just a generation past slavery; a time when there were no cars on the road or planes in the sky; when someone like her couldn't vote for two reasons—because she was a woman and because of the color of her skin. And tonight, I think about all that she's seen throughout her century in America—the heartache and the hope; the struggle and the progress; the times we were told that we can't, and the people who pressed on with that American creed: Yes, we can.

At a time when women's voices were silenced and their hopes dismissed, she lived to see them stand up and speak out and reach for the ballot. Yes, we can.

When there was despair in the Dust Bowl and depression across the land, she saw a nation conquer fear itself with a New Deal, new jobs, and a new sense of common purpose. Yes, we can.

"I was never the likeliest candidate for this office. We didn't start with much money or many endorsements. Our campaign was not hatched in the halls of Washington—it began in the backyards of Des Moines and the living rooms of Concord and the front porches of Charleston."

ANASTASIA SOMOZA

Anastasia Somoza is an International Disability Rights Advocate.

I t was 2004 in Boston when I had the honor and privilege of attending the Democratic National Convention as an at-large delegate for presidential candidate John Kerry. The political energy on the convention floor was palpable, but as a 20-year-old college student, I must admit that my attention was drawn to more trivial details. Usually dignified men and women were swirling around me in red, white, and blue Abe Lincoln–style top hats, their button collections jangling as they boogied and brimmed with progressive pride to the pop hits of that summer.

Then Senator Barack Obama took to the stage, and declared, "It's not enough for just some of us to prosper— for alongside our famous individualism, there's another ingredient in the American saga—a belief that we are all connected as one people."

"Yes!" I screamed, throwing my hands in the air as the party that had engulfed me suddenly evaporated. There was an undeniable power in his voice: It filled the atmosphere as he continued, "It's what allows us to pursue our individual dreams, yet

still come together as one American family. . . . There's not a liberal America and a conservative America— there's the United States of America."

Utterly mesmerized, I realized these words would be pivotal not only to me but to the whole country. He then asked, "Do we participate in a politics of cynicism, or do we participate in a politics of hope?" "Hope" he averred, answering his own question.

Surrounded by the cream of the crop in liberal democratic politics, I was certainly a far cry from political insider: a woman with a disability, the daughter of immigrants—yet it seemed he was speaking directly to me, challenging me to chase my dreams. I felt his words in my bones, "Hope in the face of difficulty. Hope in the face of uncertainty. The audacity of hope!" In that moment I knew I was witnessing history and that Senator Barack Obama would one day be president.

Ten years later, heart soaring with pride and joy, I was shaking President Obama's hand. I used the opportunity to express my boundless gratitude for the remarkable success his administration achieved in making Americans with disabilities more visible

with greater degrees of independence and inclusion in education, employment, and countless other aspects of everyday social life— including employing people with disabilities at the White House.

Never did I imagine that his improbable presence at the 2004 convention would see me wheeling onto that very same stage to address the party's delegates as an International Disability Rights Advocate. In 2016, we were living history together again in Philadelphia, when Hillary Clinton was nominated as the first female candidate for

president of the United States. In his eloquent paraphrasing of Teddy Roosevelt, Obama motivated me to believe that like Hillary, I too had been "that woman in the arena" and that I should never stop "striving valiantly" in my commitment to improving the lives of others.

———

Above:
THE NEW YORK- published *Irish Voice* **newspaper celebrates Anastasia Somoza's speech at the Democratic National Convention in Philadelphia, July 25, 2016.**

When the bombs fell on our harbor and tyranny threatened the world, she was there to witness a generation rise to greatness and a democracy was saved. Yes, we can.

She was there for the buses in Montgomery, the hoses in Birmingham, a bridge in Selma, and a preacher from Atlanta who told a people that "We Shall Overcome." Yes, we can.

A man touched down on the moon, a wall came down in Berlin, a world was connected by our own science and imagination. And this year, in this election, she touched her finger to a screen and cast her vote, because after 106 years in America, through the best of times and the darkest of hours, she knows how America can change. Yes, we can.

America, we have come so far. We have seen so much. But there is so much more to do. So tonight, let us ask ourselves—if our children should live to see the next

century; if my daughters should be so lucky to live as long as Ann Nixon Cooper, what change will they see? What progress will we have made?

This is our chance to answer that call. This is our moment. This is our time—to put our people back to work and open doors of opportunity for our kids; to restore prosperity and promote the cause of peace; to reclaim the American Dream and reaffirm that fundamental truth—that out of many, we are one; that while we breathe, we hope, and where we are met with cynicism and doubt and those who tell us that we can't, we will respond with that timeless creed that sums up the spirit of a people:

Yes, we can. Thank you, God bless you, and may God Bless the United States of America. ★

Above:
"YES, WE CAN": Barack Obama delivers his election night victory speech in Grant Park, Chicago, November 4, 2008.

Following pages:
THE OBAMAS wave to the enormous crowd at the inaguration.

INAUGURAL ADDRESS

January 20, 2009 | WASHINGTON, D.C.

My FELLOW CITIZENS: I stand here today humbled by the task before us, grateful for the trust you've bestowed, mindful of the sacrifices borne by our ancestors.

I thank President Bush for his service to our nation—as well as the generosity and cooperation he has shown throughout this transition.

Forty-four Americans have now taken the presidential oath. The words have been spoken during rising tides of prosperity and the still waters of peace. Yet, every so often, the oath is taken amidst gathering clouds and raging storms. At these moments, America has carried on not simply because of the skill or vision of those in high office, but because we, the people, have remained faithful to the ideals of our forebears and true to our founding documents.

So it has been; so it must be with this generation of Americans.

That we are in the midst of crisis is now well understood. Our nation is at war against a far-reaching network of violence and hatred. Our economy is badly weakened, a consequence of greed and irresponsibility on the part of some, but also our collective failure to make hard choices and prepare the nation for a new age. Homes have been lost, jobs shed, businesses shuttered. Our health care is too costly, our schools fail too many—and each day brings further evidence that the ways we use energy strengthen our adversaries and threaten our planet.

FLAG-WAVING CROWDS watch Obama give his inaugural address, January 20, 2009.

These are the indicators of crisis, subject to data and statistics. Less measurable, but no less profound, is a sapping of confidence across our land; a nagging fear that America's decline is inevitable, that the next generation must lower its sights.

Today I say to you that the challenges we face are real. They are serious and they are many. They will not be met easily or in a short span of time. But know this America: they will be met.

On this day, we gather because we have chosen hope over fear, unity of purpose over conflict and discord. On this day, we come to proclaim an end to the petty grievances and false promises, the recriminations and worn-out dogmas that for far too long have strangled our politics. We remain a young nation. But in the words of Scripture, the time has come to set aside childish things. The time has come to reaffirm our enduring spirit; to choose our better history; to carry forward that precious gift, that noble idea passed on from generation to generation: the God-given promise that all are equal, all are free, and all deserve a chance to pursue their full measure of happiness.

In reaffirming the greatness of our nation we understand that greatness is never a given. It must be earned. Our journey has never been one of short-cuts or settling

Opposite and above:
DESPITE IT BEING one of the coldest inauguration days on record, an estimated 1.8 million attended—more than double the previous record set at Bill Clinton's 1993 swearing in.

for less. It has not been the path for the faint-hearted, for those that prefer leisure over work, or seek only the pleasures of riches and fame. Rather, it has been the risk-takers, the doers, the makers of things—some celebrated but more often men and women obscure in their labor—who have carried us up the long rugged path towards prosperity and freedom.

For us, they packed up their few worldly possessions and traveled across oceans in search of a new life. For us, they toiled in sweatshops, and settled the West, endured the lash of the whip, and plowed the hard earth. For us, they fought and died in places like Concord and Gettysburg, Normandy and Khe Sahn.

Time and again these men and women struggled and sacrificed and worked till their hands were raw so that we might live a better life. They saw America as bigger than the sum of our individual ambitions, greater than all the differences of birth or wealth or faction.

THE FIRST FAMILIES viewed through a bulletproof glass screen at the inauguration on January 20, 2009.

This is the journey we continue today. We remain the most prosperous, powerful nation on Earth. Our workers are no less productive than when this crisis began. Our minds are no less inventive, our goods and services no less needed than they were last week, or last month, or last year. Our capacity remains undiminished. But our time of standing pat, of protecting narrow interests and putting off unpleasant decisions—that time has surely passed. Starting today, we must pick ourselves up, dust ourselves off, and begin again the work of remaking America.

For everywhere we look, there is work to be done. The state of our economy calls for action, bold and swift. And we will act, not only to create new jobs but to lay a new foundation for growth. We will build the roads and bridges, the electric grids and digital lines that feed our commerce and bind us together. We'll restore science to its rightful place and wield technology's wonders to raise health care's quality and lower its cost. We will harness the sun and the winds and the soil to fuel our cars and run our factories. And we will transform our schools and colleges and universities to meet the demands of a new age. All this we can do. All this we will do.

Now, there are some who question the scale of our ambitions, who suggest that our system cannot tolerate too many big plans. Their memories are short, for they have forgotten what this country has already done, what free men and women can achieve when imagination is joined to common purpose and necessity to courage. What the cynics fail to understand is that the ground has shifted beneath them, that the stale political arguments that have consumed us for so long no longer apply.

The question we ask today is not whether our government is too big or too small, but whether it works—whether it helps families find jobs at a decent wage, care they can afford, a retirement that is dignified. Where the answer is yes, we intend to move forward. Where the answer is no, programs will end. And those of us who manage the public's dollars will be held to account, to spend wisely, reform bad habits, and do our business in the light of day, because only then can we restore the vital trust between a people and their government.

Nor is the question before us whether the market is a force for good or ill. Its power to generate wealth and expand freedom is unmatched. But this crisis has reminded us that without a watchful eye, the market can spin out of control. The nation cannot prosper long when it favors only the prosperous. The success of our economy has always depended not just on the size of our gross domestic product but on the reach of our prosperity, on the ability to extend opportunity to every willing heart—not out of charity but because it is the surest route to our common good.

As for our common defense, we reject as false the choice between our safety and our ideals. Our Founding Fathers—faced with perils that we can scarcely imagine, drafted a charter to assure the rule of law and the rights of man—a charter expanded by the blood of generations. Those ideals still light the world, and we will not give them up for expedience sake.

"Our challenges may be new. The instruments with which we meet them may be new. But those values upon which our success depends—honesty and hard work, courage and fair play, tolerance and curiosity, loyalty and patriotism—these things are old. These things are true. They have been the quiet force of progress throughout our history."

And so, to all the other peoples and governments who are watching today, from the grandest capitals to the small village where my father was born, know that America is a friend of each nation and every man, woman, and child who seeks a future of peace and dignity. And we are ready to lead once more.

Recall that earlier generations faced down fascism and communism not just with missiles and tanks but with the sturdy alliances and enduring convictions. They understood that our power alone cannot protect us, nor does it entitle us to do as we please. Instead they knew that our power grows through its prudent use; our security emanates from the justness of our cause, the force of our example, the tempering qualities of humility and restraint.

We are the keepers of this legacy. Guided by these principles once more we can meet those new threats that demand even greater effort, even greater cooperation and understanding between nations. We will begin to responsibly leave Iraq to its people and forge a hard-earned peace in Afghanistan. With old friends and former foes, we'll work tirelessly to lessen the nuclear threat, and roll back the specter of a warming planet.

We will not apologize for our way of life, nor will we waver in its defense. And for those who seek to advance their aims by inducing terror and slaughtering innocents, we say to you now that our spirit is stronger and cannot be broken—you cannot outlast us, and we will defeat you.

For we know that our patchwork heritage is a strength, not a weakness. We are a nation of Christians and Muslims, Jews and Hindus, and non-believers. We are shaped by every language and culture, drawn from every end of this Earth; and because we have tasted the bitter swill of civil war and segregation, and emerged from that dark chapter stronger and more united, we cannot help but believe that the old hatreds shall someday pass; that the lines of tribe shall soon dissolve; that as the world grows smaller our common humanity shall reveal itself; and that America must play its role in ushering in a new era of peace.

To the Muslim world, we seek a new way forward, based on mutual interest and mutual respect. To those leaders around the globe who seek to sow conflict or blame their society's ills on the West, know that your people will judge you on what you can build, not what you destroy.

To those who cling to power through corruption and deceit and the silencing of dissent, know that you are on the wrong side of history, but that we will extend a hand if you are willing to unclench your fist.

To the people of poor nations, we pledge to work alongside you to make your farms flourish and let clean waters flow; to nourish starved bodies and feed hungry minds. And to those nations like ours that enjoy relative plenty, we say we can no longer afford indifference to the suffering outside our borders, nor can we consume the world's resources without regard to effect. For the world has changed, and we must change with it.

"Let it be said by our children's children, that when we were tested we refused to let this journey end, that we did not turn back, nor did we falter; and with eyes fixed on the horizon and God's grace upon us, we carried forth that great gift of freedom and delivered it safely to future generations."

As we consider the role that unfolds before us, we remember with humble gratitude those brave Americans who at this very hour patrol far-off deserts and distant mountains. They have something to tell us, just as the fallen heroes who lie in Arlington whisper through the ages.

We honor them not only because they are the guardians of our liberty, but because they embody the spirit of service—a willingness to find meaning in something greater than themselves.

And yet at this moment, a moment that will define a generation, it is precisely this spirit that must inhabit us all. For as much as government can do, and must do, it is ultimately the faith and determination of the American people upon which this nation relies. It is the kindness to take in a stranger when the levees break, the selflessness of workers who would rather cut their hours than see a friend lose their job, which sees us through our darkest hours. It is the firefighter's courage to storm a stairway filled with smoke, but also a parent's willingness to nurture a child, that finally decides our fate.

Our challenges may be new. The instruments with which we meet them may be new. But those values upon which our success depends—honesty and hard work, courage and fair play, tolerance and curiosity, loyalty and patriotism—these things are old. These things are true. They have been the quiet force of progress throughout our history.

What is demanded, then, is a return to these truths. What is required of us now is a new era of responsibility—a recognition on the part of every American that we have

ON A DAY they will remember for the rest of their lives—two junior newshounds take to the air to tell their stories.

duties to ourselves, our nation, and the world; duties that we do not grudgingly accept but rather seize gladly, firm in the knowledge that there is nothing so satisfying to the spirit, so defining of our character, than giving our all to a difficult task.

This is the price and the promise of citizenship. This is the source of our confidence—the knowledge that God calls on us to shape an uncertain destiny. This is the meaning of our liberty and our creed, why men and women and children of every race and every faith can join in celebration across this magnificent mall; and why a man whose father less than 60 years ago might not have been served in a local restaurant can now stand before you to take a most sacred oath.

So let us mark this day with remembrance of who we are and how far we have traveled. In the year of America's birth, in the coldest of months, a small band of patriots huddled by dying campfires on the shores of an icy river. The capital was abandoned. The enemy was advancing. The snow was stained with blood. At the moment when the outcome of our revolution was most in doubt, the father of our nation ordered these words to be read to the people:

"Let it be told to the future world, that in the depth of winter, when nothing but hope and virtue could survive, that the city and the country, alarmed at one common danger, came forth to meet [it]."

America: in the face of our common dangers, in this winter of our hardship, let us remember these timeless words. With hope and virtue, let us brave once more the icy currents, and endure what storms may come. Let it be said by our children's children that, when we were tested, we refused to let this journey end; that we did not turn back, nor did we falter; and with eyes fixed on the horizon and God's grace upon us, we carried forth that great gift of freedom and delivered it safely to future generations. Thank you. God bless you. And God bless the United States of America. ★

AT THE PARIS Hotel de Ville (Town Hall), a sellout expat crowd celebrates the inauguration with appropriate joie de vivre.

FIRSTS

President BORN OUTSIDE OF THE 48 CONTIGUOUS STATES
and FIRST BORN IN HAWAII

★

AFRICAN AMERICAN *to serve as president*

★

MULTIRACIAL AMERICAN *to serve as president*

★

President to APPOINT A HISPANIC AMERICAN TO THE SUPREME COURT

★

President to APPOINT MULTIPLE WOMEN TO THE SUPREME COURT

★

President to HAVE A CATHOLIC VICE PRESIDENT (JOE BIDEN)

★

President to TO ADDRESS BOTH HOUSES OF THE BRITISH PARLIAMENT

★

President to VISIT A FEDERAL PRISON

★

President to VISIT HIROSHIMA

★

Sitting President to PUBLISH A SCIENTIFIC PAPER

★

President to HAVE HIS OFFICIAL PHOTOGRAPHIC PORTRAIT TAKEN
WITH A DIGITAL CAMERA

★

Sitting President to HAVE BEEN THE KEYNOTE SPEAKER AT A
DEMOCRATIC NATIONAL CONVENTION

★

President to HAVE HIS OWN TWITTER HANDLE—@POTUS

THE WAY FORWARD

"The first hundred days is going to be important, but it's probably going to be the first thousand days that makes the difference." —BARACK OBAMA, **October 2008**

In 2008, when Barack Obama became the first democrat in over three decades to win more than half of the popular vote, the country—or, for that matter, the world—he inherited was in the midst of a catastrophic economic meltdown.

He was greeted with U.S. unemployment at 7.8 percent and it was rapidly worsening at a calamitous clip of over 700,000 jobs a month: in 2009, Fortune 500 companies alone would eliminate almost a million jobs. Capital markets were frozen, banks weren't lending, consumers weren't spending, and industry was suffering. One of the biggest, the U.S. auto industry, was on the brink of bankruptcy: unit production was down some 40 percent over the preceding two years, and millions more jobs at suppliers and dealerships were threatened. Even some of Wall Street's oldest most venerable names were allowed to disappear while others were forced into new improbable "shotgun" marriages.

Faced with this disaster, the new commander in chief and his senior team's way forward called for a lot more than "the audacity of hope." They now needed to summon up the raw courage to expeditiously make a range of difficult, and often controversial, economic decisions. The first task was to drive the biggest stimulus bill ever enacted—over $800 billion—through Congress.

Congress was the other 800-pound gorilla, one that only a bold and determined leader with a highly seasoned team could stare down and wrestle to the mat. Of course, there would be a price to pay. In October 2013, Congress would shut down the government for 15 days to delay and defund the Patient Protection and Affordable Care Act—a shutdown that Standard & Poor's stated took $24 billion out of the economy. And so the internecine battle would go for the full eight years of the Obama presidency. ★

Previous pages:
ON HIS FIRST day on the job, before the president sits down at his Oval Office desk, some 4,000 political appointees had to be put in place behind the scenes.

Opposite:
FIRST DOG BO takes the president for his morning constitutional in the East Colonnade of the White House, March 15, 2009.

SENATE AND CONGRESSIONAL House
Leaders break bread in the White House in
hopes of breaking the deadlock, May 16, 2012.

TWEED ROOSEVELT

Tweed Roosevelt *is a great-grandson of Theodore Roosevelt and the chairman of Roosevelt China Investments, a Boston-based company.*

It is well known that my great-grandfather, Theodore Roosevelt, had an excellent sense of humor, although examples are mostly unrecorded. In February 2012, my daughter and I went to the White House to visit President Obama in the Oval Office on the occasion of his giving my stepmother Selwa "Lucky" Roosevelt a commendation for her long work as chief of protocol. She led the effort to restore Blair House, the presidential guest house. I happily learned that President Obama had an endearing sense of humor as well. Two stories from that visit will illustrate the point.

Before I arrived, I had planned an icebreaker. When I got a chance, I told him I had just returned from Cuba and I wanted him to know that I had tried to bring him some Cuban cigars. I told him that customs had found the cigars and were going to confiscate them. "Mr. President," I said, "I told customs the cigars were for you but they seemed unimpressed, and they took them anyway."

"Tweed," he said, "don't worry about it. I have my own sources."

I have often wondered if he knew I had made up the story, knowing about his battle with tobacco, and I certainly did not take his response seriously. A little later the president said, "Tweed, I want to show you something." He took me to a small closet-like room that might have been a wet bar and pointed at a photograph on the wall. It was of an elderly TR in outdoor gear dragging a reluctant horse up a steep incline. "That photograph," he said, "was given to me by a cousin of yours who said that it was one of TR's favorite pictures, because it reminded him of his dealings with Congress." He paused as I looked at it, and then said:

"I feel exactly the same way." We had a good laugh and then went on with the ceremony for my stepmother.

It occurs to me that a lesson I learned on a remote river high in the Amazon while retracing TR's River of Doubt expedition is relevant. After my adventure, I was often asked what is the one essential thing to take along on a dangerous and difficult adventure. The answer was clear to me: what one needs most is a sense of humor. Being president is an undertaking most dangerous and difficult, and if you want someone who is up to the job, one of the criteria ought to be someone who can laugh. If you look back in history, I think you will find that all successful presidents loved a good joke. This is certainly true for TR and Obama— both extraordinary presidents.

———

Above:
TEDDY ROOSEVELT and his horse near the Grand Canyon in Arizona, 1913.

Opposite, above: **AFTER A WHITE** House lunch, the president jokingly demonstrates to Senator Bernie Sanders the big difference between a glass half full and a glass half empty.

Opposite, below: **AFTER SIGNING THE** Fair Sentencing Act in the Oval Office on August 3, 2010, President Obama shares a lighthearted moment with members of Congress; (l-r): Attorney General Eric Holder, Sen. Patrick Leahy (D-VT), Rep. Bobby Scott (D-VA), Senate Majority Whip Richard Durbin (D-IL), Sen. Orrin Hatch (R-UT), Sen. Jeff Sessions (R-AL), Rep. Sheila Jackson-Lee (D-TX), and Sen. Lindsey Graham (R-SC).

LISTENING TO AMERICA

IT STARTED WITH a phone call from the Mayor of Columbus, Ohio, to ask if Rhonda and Joe Weithman and their family might be interested in attending an event at which President Obama would be speaking. This morphed, however, into what Rhonda describes as, "the most incredible experience of our lives." Rather than the Weithmans going to see the president, the president would be coming to see them!

Three days later, after making friends with the advance team of Secret Service agents, the president was walking through their front door. Said Rhonda, "He immediately shook hands with our kids and put everyone at ease." The president then sat down for a full 30 minutes with the Weithmans at their kitchen table. "He didn't for a moment make us feel like this was just a photo op. I've heard it said that he's cold and aloof, but I couldn't disagree more," said Rhonda. "He came across as just a regular guy who's ready to listen and genuinely wants to make things

better." Next, it was outside to the backyard, where 40 neighbors were waiting in lawn chairs, and for the next 45 minutes, "Lots of real questions were asked and answered."

But then the Weithman children, Rachel, 9, and Josh, 11, surprised everyone with a question they'd been saving for the president. Would he do the OHIO sign with them? The Leader of the Free World laughingly agreed, saying, "Sure, but what letter do you want me to be?" He laughed even harder when it was pointed out that obviously he had to be "The Big O."

"The greatest legacy from the visit," said Rhonda, "was the heightened political awareness it engendered in our kids and the sense that we do have a voice." ★

Opposite, above and inset: PRESIDENT OBAMA WITH the Weithman family in their kitchen; "making" the OHIO sign.

Above, clockwise from left: THE PRESIDENT TALKS with people at the Grasshoppers store in LeClaire, Iowa, during a three-day bus tour in the Midwest, August 16, 2011; on the same day, the president has breakfast with small business owners at Rausch's Café in Guttenberg, Iowa; the president, seated between Steve Jobs of Apple and Facebook founder Mark Zuckerberg, toasts the titans of the digital age in San Francisco, February 2011. Others attending the dinner included Google CEO Eric Schmidt, Yahoo! CEO Carol Bartz, Twitter CEO Dick Costolo, Oracle CEO Larry Ellison, and Netflix CEO Reed Hastings.

BY THE NUMBERS, 2009–2016:

HOMICIDES -13%

★

VIOLENT CRIMES -16%

★

GUN BUYER CHECKS +58%

★

JOBS CREATED +10 million

★

JOB OPENINGS +97%

★

UNEMPLOYMENT *December 2016* 4.6% *Down from* 8.5% *in March 2009*

★

CORPORATE PROFITS +166%

★

EXPORTS OF GOODS AND SERVICES +31%

★

NEW CAR MPG +19%

★

S&P 500 +139%

★

UNINSURED -15.3%

★

U.S. CRUDE OIL PRODUCTION +87%

★

PETROLEUM IMPORTS -62%

★

WIND AND SOLAR POWER +273%

★

NATURALIZATIONS *Approximately* 5.6 million

★

BABIES BORN *Approximately* 30 million

SAVING THE AUTO INDUSTRY

ON NOVEMBER 18, 2008, despite his Motor City hometown roots, Mitt Romney wrote an op-ed article for the *New York Times* titled "Let Detroit Go Bankrupt." The opening paragraph read: *If General Motors, Ford and Chrysler get the bailout that their chief executives asked for yesterday, you can kiss the American automotive industry goodbye. It won't go overnight, but its demise will be virtually guaranteed.*

Barack Obama saw things differently. In the final weeks of the George W. Bush administration, a few emergency bridge loans were issued to the auto industry, but Detroit's salvation came by the hand of the newly elected president. Flying in the face of legions of naysayers, in spring 2009 Obama implemented an aggressive $80 billion loan package that included the government taking a 60 percent ownership stake in GM. According to an analysis by the Center for Automotive Research, doing so saved as many as four million direct and indirect auto industry-related jobs and $105 billion in costs to Americans.

While the final net cost to taxpayers on the actual $80 billion loan was calculated to be $9.7 billion, this figure does not take into consideration all the related economic upsides, such as the impact of millions of workers in good jobs paying taxes. But no matter what metric one uses, Obama's so-called "bailout" worked. The U.S. auto industry was pulled back from the edge of the precipice. Since those dark days, the industry has staged a remarkable recovery and is flourishing. According to J.D. Power, 2016 sales reached a record number of 17.5 million units—an astonishing increase of 68 percent since 2009.

In June 2009, House Minority Leader John Boehner contemptuously asked: "Does anyone really believe that politicians and bureaucrats in Washington can successfully steer a multinational corporation to economic viability?" Well, to quote Barack Obama, the answer, was "Yes we can" and, in retrospect, "Yes we did." ★

MEMBERS OF THE auto industry task force meet as President Obama mans the phone, March 29, 2009, the night before he announced his plans for GM and Chrysler.

And now, here we are a year later, GM, Chrysler, and Ford are all posting a profit. The U.S. auto industry has hired 55,000 workers—the most job growth in a decade. And not only that, but you're producing the cars of the future right here at this plant, cars that are going to reduce our dependence on foreign oil. This car right here doesn't need a sip of gasoline for 40 miles and then keeps on going after that."

—BARACK OBAMA to GM workers, July 30, 2010

PRESIDENT OBAMA ADDRESSES workers at
the GM Detroit-Hamtramck Assembly Center in
Hamtramck, Michigan, July 30, 2010.

THANK
YOU

EALTHCARE.BARACKOBAMA.COM

ON THE AFFORDABLE CARE ACT

October 20, 2016 | MIAMI-DADE COLLEGE, MIAMI, FLORIDA [ABRIDGED]

ELLO, MIAMI! Thank you so much. Well, everybody have a seat. It is good to see all of you! It's good to be back at Miami-Dade! One of my favorite institutions! Love this school.

I want to thank your longtime president and great friend, Eduardo J. Padrón. And to all the faculty and staff, and of course most importantly, the students, for hosting me—I want to say how grateful I am. I want to thank the wonderful elected officials who are here today. I'm going to just point out two outstanding members of Congress—Debbie Wasserman Schultz—and Ted Deutch. . . .

The first thing I want to say is thank you for your support, and thank you for the opportunity and the privilege you've given me to serve these past eight years. I remember standing just a few blocks north of here in the closing days of the 2008 campaign. And at that point, we were already realizing that we were in the midst of the worst economic crisis of our lifetimes. We didn't know where the bottom would be. We were still in the middle of two wars. Over 150,000 of our troops were overseas. But thanks to the hard work and the determination of the American people, when I come here today the story is different.

Working together, we've cut the unemployment rate in Florida by more than half. Across the country, we turned years of job losses into the longest streak of job creation on record. We slashed our

MEMBERS OF THE crowd listen as President Obama delivers remarks on Medicaid fraud and health-care reform at St. Charles High School in St. Charles, Missouri, March 10, 2010.

dependence on foreign oil, doubled our production of renewable energy. Incomes are rising again, they rose more last year than any time ever recorded. Poverty is falling. It fell more last year than any time since 1968. Our graduation rates from high school are at record highs. College enrollment is significantly higher than it was when we came into office. Marriage equality is a reality in all 50 states.

So we've been busy. This is why I've got gray hair. But we did one other thing. We fought to make sure that in America, health care is not just a privilege, but a right for every single American. And that's what I want to talk about here today.

You've heard a lot about Obamacare, as it's come to be known. You heard a lot about it in the six and a half years since I signed it into law. And some of the things you heard might even be true. But one thing I want to start with is just reminding people why it is that we fought for health reform in the first place. Because it was one of the key motivators in my campaign.

And it wasn't just because rising health costs were eating into workers' paychecks and straining budgets for businesses and for governments. It wasn't just because before the law was passed, insurance companies could just drop your coverage because you got sick, right at the time you needed insurance most.

It was because of you. It was because of the stories that I was hearing all around the country and right here in Florida—hearing from people who had been forced to fight a broken health-care system at the same time as they were fighting to get well.

Above:
OBAMA MEETS WITH Senate Democrats at the White House to discuss health-care reform, June 2, 2009.

Opposite:
LISTENING DURING a Health Care Summit session in the East Room of the White House, March 5, 2009; front row, (l-r): White House Domestic Policy Council Director Melody Barnes, Sen. Ted Kennedy (D-MA), Sen. Max Baucus (D-MT), and Rep. Charles Rangel (D-NY).

It was about children like Zoe Lihn, who needed heart surgery when she was just 15 hours old. And she was already halfway to hitting her lifetime insurance cap before she was old enough to walk. Her parents had no idea how they could possibly make sure that she continued to make progress. And today, because of the Affordable Care Act, Zoe is in first grade, and she's loving martial arts, and she's got a bright future ahead of her.

"It was because of you. It was because of the stories that I was hearing all around the country."

We fought so hard for health reform because of women like Amanda Heidel, who lives here in South Florida. As a girl, she was diagnosed with diabetes—a disease with costs that can add up quickly if you don't have insurance, can eat away at your dreams. But thanks to the Affordable Care Act, Amanda got to stay on her parents' plan after college. When she turned 26, Amanda went online, she shopped for an affordable health-insurance plan that covered her medications. Today, she's pursuing a doctorate in psychology. And Amanda said that the Affordable Care Act "has given me the security and freedom to choose how I live my life." That's what this was all about.

Zoe and Amanda, the people who I get letters from every single day describing what it meant not to fear that if they got sick, or a member of their family got sick, if they, heaven forbid, were in an accident, that somehow they could lose everything.

So because of this law, because of Obamacare, another 20 million Americans now know the financial security of health insurance. So do another three million children, thanks in large part to the Affordable Care Act and the improvements, the

AMY WILHITE

Amy Wilhite *is a volunteer for the American Cancer Society Action Network and the mother of* Taylor Wilhite.

My daughter, Taylor, was just eight years old when she was diagnosed with acute myeloid leukemia, which is a rapidly progressing cancer of the blood and bone marrow. Her treatment included multiple rounds of intense chemotherapy followed by a bone marrow transplant.

Obviously, our world was turned upside down, and our single focus in life became doing everything in our power to get Taylor cured. I was surprised when a social worker told me about the "lifetime maximums" that some insurance policies featured: I had never heard of such a thing but, on checking our plan, was horrified to discover that Taylor did in fact have a lifetime coverage cap.

This meant that by age nine, Taylor was going to exhaust the value they had assigned to her and we would be on our own to battle her cancer without insurance. We thought our family had done everything right. Taylor's father was employed, carried insurance on her, and paid the premiums. However, in the small print, the insurance

policy had a limit on the how much they'd cover over the course of her lifetime, and when that was reached, they could stop paying her medical bills.

What were we to do? If we tried to get another insurance policy for our little girl, she would either be uninsurable due to a preexisting

condition, or the premiums would be ridiculously high and way beyond our means. Our only hope was the pending passage of the Affordable Care Act.

In desperation, I reached out to President Obama with an email to the White House. I told him how urgent it was that he continue to push

the ACA and encouraged him to fight for our daughter and others facing the same dilemma. I needed our voice to be heard and it was.

After the bill's passage, Taylor and I were invited to attend a White House event celebrating its signing, where, after telling our story to the other guests, I had the incredible privilege of introducing the President of the United States and thanking him personally on national television. President Obama may not be a doctor, but he did help save my daughter's life through the passage of the Affordable Care Act, and for this we will be eternally grateful.

Taylor is now a healthy 18-year-old attending college and studying psychology. She plans to work as a child life specialist with pediatric hospital patients, giving back to others and proving that life is indeed priceless.

Above:
AMY WILHITE and her daughter, Taylor, meet with President Obama following his remarks on the 90-day anniversary of the signing of the Affordable Care Act, in the East Room of the White House, June 22, 2010.

enhancements that we made to the Children's Health Insurance Program. And the net result is that never in American history has the uninsured rate been lower than it is today. Never. And that's true across the board. It's dropped among women, among Latinos and African Americans, every other demographic group. It's worked.

Now, that doesn't mean that it's perfect. No law is. . . . But we've also always known—and I have always said—that for all the good that the Affordable Care Act is doing right now—for as big a step forward as it was—it's still just a first step. It's like building a starter home, or buying a starter home. It's a lot better than not having a home, but you hope that over time you make some improvements. And in fact, since we first signed the law, we've already taken a number of steps to improve it. And we can do even more—but only if we put aside all the political rhetoric, all the partisanship, and just be honest about what's working, what needs fixing, and how we fix it.

So that's what I want to do today. . . . I might get into the details. I hope you don't mind. Let's start with a basic fact. The majority of Americans do not get health care through the Affordable Care Act. Eighty percent or so of Americans get health care on the job, through their employer, or . . . through Medicaid, or . . . through Medicare. And so for most Americans, the Affordable Care Act has not affected your coverage—except to make it stronger.

Because of the law, you now have free preventive care. Insurance companies have to offer that in whatever policy they sell. Because of the law, you now have free checkups for women. Because of the law, you get free mammograms. Because of the

THE AUDIENCE LISTENS closely as the president addresses a town hall meeting on health-care reform at Gallatin Field in Belgrade, Montana, August 14, 2009.

law, it is harder for insurance companies to discriminate against you because you're a woman when you get health insurance. Because of the law, doctors are finding better ways to perform heart surgeries, and delivering healthier babies, and treating chronic disease, and reducing the number of people that, once they're in the hospital, end up having to return to the hospital. So you're getting better quality even though you don't know that Obamacare is doing it. Thanks, Obama.

Because of the law, your annual out-of-pocket spending is capped. Seniors get discounts on their prescription drugs because of the law. Young people can stay on their parents' plan—just like Amanda did—because of the law. And Amanda was able to stay on her parents' plan and then get insurance after she aged out, even though she has what used to be called a preexisting condition—because we made it illegal to discriminate against people with preexisting conditions.

By the way, before this law, before Obamacare, health insurance rates for everybody . . . were going up really fast. This law has actually slowed down the pace of health-care inflation. So every year premiums have gone up, but they've gone up the slowest in 50 years since Obamacare was passed. In fact, if your family gets insurance through your job, your family is paying, on average, about $3,600 less per year than you would be if the cost trends that had existed before the law were passed had continued. . . . That's money in your pocket.

PRESIDENT OBAMA REVIEWS the edits to the edits of his speech on health care in preparation for his address to a joint session of Congress, September 9, 2009.

Now, some people may say, well, I've seen my copays go up, or my networks have changed. But these are decisions that are made by your employers. It's not because of Obamacare. They're not determined by the Affordable Care Act.

So if Obamacare hasn't changed the coverage of the 80 percent of Americans who already had insurance, except to make it a better value [and] more reliable, how has the law impacted the other 15 or 20 percent of Americans who didn't have health insurance through their job, or didn't qualify for Medicaid or Medicare?

Well, before the Affordable Care Act, frankly, you were probably out of luck. Either you had to buy health insurance on your own, because you weren't getting it through the job, and it was wildly expensive, and your premiums were going up all the time, and if you happened to get sick and use the insurance, the next year the insurer could drop you. And if you had had an illness like cancer or diabetes or some other chronic disease, you couldn't buy new insurance because the insurance company's attitude was, you know what, this is just going to cost us money, we don't want to insure you.

So if you were trying to buy health insurance on your own, it was either hugely expensive or didn't provide very effective coverage. You might buy a policy thinking that it was going to cover you. It was sort of like when I was young and I bought my first car, I had to buy car insurance . . . because it was the law. I got the cheapest one I could get, because I didn't have any money—and it was a really beat-up car. And I remember somebody rear-ends me, and I call up the insurance company thinking maybe I can get some help, and they laughed at me. They're all like, "what, are you kidding?" It didn't provide any coverage other than essentially allowing me to drive.

Well, that's what it was like for a lot of people who didn't have health insurance on the job. So that meant that a lot of people just didn't bother getting health insurance at all. And when they got sick, they'd have to go to the emergency room—. . . the most expensive place to get care. And because you weren't insured, the hospital would have to give you the care for free, and they would have to then make up for those costs by charging everybody else more money. So it wasn't good for anybody.

What the Affordable Care Act is designed to do is to help those people who were previously either uninsured or underinsured. And it worked to help those people in two ways. First, we gave states funding to expand Medicaid to cover more people. In D.C. and the 31 states that took us up on that, more than 4 million people have coverage who didn't have it before. They now have health insurance.

Second, for people who made too much to qualify for Medicaid even after we expanded it, we set up what we call "marketplaces" on HealthCare.gov, so you could shop for a plan that fits your needs, and then we would give you tax credits to help you buy it. And most people today can find a plan for less than $75 a month at the HealthCare.gov marketplace when you include the tax credits that government is

"So . . . why is there still such a fuss? Well, part of the problem is the fact that a Democratic president named Barack Obama passed the law. And that's just the truth. I mean, I worked really, really hard to engage Republicans; took Republican ideas that originally they had praised; said, 'let's work together. . . .' And when they just refused to do anything, we said, 'all right, we're going to have to do it with Democrats.' And that's what we did."

giving you. That means it's less than your cellphone bill—because I know you guys are tweeting a lot—and texting and selfies. And the good news is, is that most people who end up buying their coverage through the marketplaces, using these tax credits, are satisfied with their plans.

So not only did Obamacare do a lot of good for the 80-plus percent of Americans who already had health care, but now it gave a new affordable option to a lot of folks who never had options before. All told, about another 10 percent of the country now have coverage.

The Affordable Care Act has done what it was designed to do: It gave us affordable health care. So what's the problem? Why is there still such a fuss? Well, part of the problem is the fact that a Democratic president named Barack Obama passed the law. And that's just the truth. I mean, I worked really, really hard to engage Republicans; took Republican ideas that originally they had praised; said, let's work together to get this done. And when they just refused to do anything, we said, all right, we're going to have to do it with Democrats. And that's what we did.

And early on, Republicans just decided to oppose it. And then they tried to scare people with all kinds of predictions—that it would be a job-killer; it would force everyone into government-run insurance; it would lead to rationing; it would lead to death panels; it would bankrupt the federal government. You remember all this. And despite the fact that all the bad things they predicted have not actually happened; despite the fact that we've created more jobs since the bill passed in consecutive months than any time on record; despite the fact that the uninsured rate has gone down to its lowest levels ever; despite that fact that it's actually cost less than anybody anticipated and has shown to be much less disruptive on existing plans that people get through their employers; despite the fact that it saved Medicare over $150 billion—which makes that program more secure—despite all this, it's been hard, if not impossible, for any Republican to admit it. . . .

So they just keep on repeating, "we're going to repeal it. We're going to repeal it, and we're going to replace it with something better"—even though, six and a half years later, they still haven't shown us what it is that they would do that would be better.

But—and this is actually the main reason I'm here—just because a lot of the Republican criticism has proven to be false and politically motivated doesn't mean that there aren't some legitimate concerns about how the law is working now. And the main issue has to do with the folks who still aren't getting enough help. Remember, I said 80 percent of people, even before the law passed, already had health insurance. And then we expanded Medicaid and set up the marketplaces, and another 10 percent of people got health insurance. That still leaves that last 10 percent; the fact that that last 10 percent still has difficulties is something we've got to do something about.

Now, part of the reason for this is, as I already mentioned, not every state expanded Medicaid to its citizens, which means that some of the most vulnerable working families that the law was designed to help still haven't gotten insurance. As you may have heard, Florida is one of those states. . . . If your governor would

Opposite, counterclockwise from top left: **THE PRESIDENT WORKING** tirelessly day and night in consultation with Paul Ryan, Nancy Pelosi, senior stakeholders from the healthcare industry, and multiple others to bring bipartisan consensus to what will become the ACA.

just put politics aside and do what's right, then more than 700,000 Floridians would suddenly have access to coverage. And, by the way, that would hold down costs for the rest of you, because there would be less uncompensated care in hospitals. And it means that people who did sign up for the marketplace, who oftentimes may be sicker, qualify for Medicaid, so they're not raising costs in the marketplace.

In fact, if the 19 states who so far have not expanded Medicaid would just do so, another 4 million people would have coverage right now all across the country.

So that's step number one. And that's, by the way, just completely in the control of these governors. They could be doing it—right now. They could do it tomorrow.

Now, the second issue has to do with the marketplaces. Although the marketplaces are working well in most of the states, there are some states where there's the marketplaces areenough competition between insurers. So if you only have one insurer, they may decide "we're going to jack up rates because we can, because nobody else is offering a better price."

In those states where the governor or legislature is hostile to the ACA, it makes it harder to enroll people because the state is not actively participating in outreach. And so, as a consequence, in those states, enrollment in the plan—especially enrollment of young people—has lagged.

And what that means is that the insurance pool is smaller and it gets a higher percentage of older and sicker people signing up—because if you're sick or you're old, you're more likely to say, "well, I'm going to sign up, no matter what, because I know I'm going to need it"; if you're young and healthy like you guys, you say, "eh, I'm fine, life is good"— . . . so you have fewer younger and healthier people signing up, and that drives rates up because the people who use health care most end up being in the insurance pool; people who use it least are not.

And then, in some cases, insurers just set their prices too low at the outset because they didn't know what the insurance pool was going to look like, and then they started losing money. And so now they've decided to significantly increase premiums in some states.

Now, it's these premium increases in some of the states in the marketplace that sometimes attracts negative headlines. Remember, these increases won't impact most of the people who are buying insurance through the marketplace, because even when premiums go up, the tax credits go up to offset the increases. So people who qualify for tax credits, they may not even notice their premiums went up because the tax credit is covered. And keep in mind that these premium increases that some of you may have read about have no effect at all if you're getting health insurance on the job or through Medicaid or Medicare. So for the 80-plus [percent of] people who already had health insurance, if your premium is going up, it's not because of Obamacare. It's because of your employer or your insurer—even though sometimes they try to blame Obamacare for why the rates go up. . . .

"But understand, no president can do it alone. We will need Republicans in Congress and in state governments to act responsibly and put politics aside. Because I want to remind you, a lot of the Affordable Care Act is built on Republican ideas."

But if you are one of the people who doesn't get health care on the job, doesn't qualify for Medicaid . . . [or] Medicare—doesn't qualify for a tax credit to help you buy insurance, because maybe you made just a little bit too much money under the law—these premium increases do make insurance less affordable. In some states, the increases are manageable. Some are 2 or 8 percent, some 20 percent. But we know there are some states that may see premiums go up by 50 percent or more.

An extreme example is Arizona, where we expect benchmark premiums will more than double. Part of this is because Arizona is one of those states that had really low average premiums—among the lowest in the country—so now insurance companies basically are trying to catch up, and they also don't have a lot of competition there. And meanwhile, in states like Florida, the failure to expand Medicaid contributes to higher marketplace premiums. And then there are some other states that just because of the nature of their health-care systems, or the fact that they're rural and people are dispersed, so it's harder to provide health care, more expensive—they have a tougher time controlling costs generally.

Again, the tax credits in the ACA will protect most consumers from the brunt of these premium increases. And with the ability to shop around on HealthCare.gov— which works really well now—most people can find plans for prices even lower than this year's prices. But there are going to be people who are hurt by premium increases or a lack of competition and choice. And I don't want to see anybody left out without health insurance. I don't want to see any family having to choose between health insurance now or saving for retirement, or saving for their kids' college education, or just paying their own bills. So the question we should be asking is, what do we do about these growing pains in the Affordable Care Act, and how do we get the last 9 percent of Americans covered? . . . And how do we make sure that premiums are

PRESIDENT OBAMA and Speaker Nancy Pelosi exchange ideas during the nationally televised bipartisan meeting reform at Blair House in Washington, D.C., February 25, 2010.

more stable going forward and the marketplace insurance pools are more stable going forward?

Well, I can tell you what will not work. Repealing the Affordable Care Act will not work. That's a bad idea. That will not solve the problem. Because right off the bat, repeal would take away health care from 20 million people. We'd go back where 80 percent of people had health insurance instead of 90 percent—right off the bat. And all the reforms that everybody benefits from that I talked about . . . would go away for everybody, because that's part of Obamacare.

"They just can't admit that a lot of good things have happened and the bad things they predicted didn't happen."

All the progress that we've made in controlling costs and improving how health care is delivered, progress that's helped hold growth in the price of health care to the slowest rate in 50 years—all that goes away. That's what "repeal" means. And the majority of Americans, even if they don't know that they're benefitting from Obamacare, don't want to see these benefits and protections taken away from their families now that they have them. I guarantee you there are people who right now think they hate Obamacare. And if somebody told them, "all right, we're repealing it, but now your kid who is on your plan is no longer on your plan," or "now you've got a preexisting condition and you can't buy health insurance"—they'd be shocked. They'd be—"what do you mean?"

So repeal is not the answer. Here is what we can do instead to actually make the ACA work even better than it's working right now. And I've already mentioned one: Florida and every state should expand Medicaid. Cover more people. It's easy to do, and it could be done right now. You'd cover 4 million more Americans, help drive down premiums for folks who buy insurance through the marketplace. And, by the way, because the federal government pays for almost all of this expansion, you can't use as an excuse that, well, the state can't afford it—because the federal government is paying it. States like Louisiana that just expanded Medicaid—you had a Republican governor replaced by a Democratic governor. He said, "I want that money." Expanded Medicaid and found not only does it insure more people, but it's actually saved the state big money and makes people less dependent on expensive emergency-room care. So that's step number one.

Step number two: since overall health-care costs have turned out to be significantly lower than everyone expected since we passed Obamacare, since that's saved the federal government billions of dollars, we should use some of that money, some of those savings, to provide more tax credits for more middle-income families, for more young adults to help them buy insurance. It will make their premiums more affordable. And that's not just good for them—it's good for everybody. Because when more people are in the marketplace, everybody will benefit from lower premiums. Healthier, younger people start joining the pool; premiums generally go down. That'd be number two.

The third thing we should do is add what's called a public plan fallback—to give folks more options in those places where there are just not enough insurers to compete. And that's especially important in some rural communities, and rural states, and counties. If you live in L.A. right now, then it's working fine. There are a lot of insurers because it's a big market, there are a lot of providers. But if you're in some remote areas, or you're near some small towns, it may be that the economics of it just don't work unless

HEALTH-CARE STOCK PRICES 2008–2017

HEALTH-CARE COMPANY/TICKER SYMBOL	JAN-22-08 *Bush president*	JAN-20-09 *Obama inauguration*	20-JAN-17 *Closing on last day of Obama presidency*	JAN-20-17 *Percentage of change*
AETNA/AET	$54.0*	$27.32*	$123.83*	+346%
ANTHEM/ANTM	73.50	37.82	150.53	+298%
CIGNA/CI	49.55	15.23	144.19	+846%
WELCARE/WCG	51.01	11.57	146.27	+1164%
UNITED HEALTH/UNH	51.50	25.41	158.43	+525%
HUMANA/HUM	80.01	33.14	201.90	+509%

*Stock prices on dates listed. Prices reflect average daily stock price for the six largest U.S. health-insurance companies on days listed except for January 20, 2017, which is the closing price and the end date of the Obama presidency.

SOURCE: Yahoo Finance–Historical Prices, *MarketWatch*

the government is providing an option to make it affordable. And, by the way, this is not complicated. Basically, you would just wait and see—if the private insurers are competing for business, then you don't have to trigger a public option. But if no private insurers are providing affordable insurance in an area, then the government would step in with a quality plan that people can afford.

And, by the way, this is not a radical idea. This idea is modeled on something that Republicans championed under George Bush for the Medicare Part D drug benefit program. It was fine when it was their idea. The fact that they're now opposed to it as some socialist scheme is not being consistent, it's being partisan.

And finally, we should continue to encourage innovation by the states. What the [ACA] says is, here's how we propose you insure your populations, but if you, the state, can figure out a different way to accomplish the same goal—providing affordable, comprehensive coverage for the same number of residents at the same cost—then go right ahead. There may be more than one way to skin a cat. Maybe you've got an idea we haven't thought of. Just show us what the plan looks like, don't talk about it.

Republicans who claim to care about your health insurance choices and your premiums but then offer nothing and block commonsense solutions like the ones that I propose to improve them—that's not right. And my message to them has been and will continue to be: work with us. Make the system better. Help the people you serve. We're open to good ideas, but they've got to be real ideas—not just slogans, not just votes to repeal. And they've got to pass basic muster. You can't say, well, if we just plant some magic beans, then everybody will have health insurance. No, we've got to have health-care economists and experts look at it and see if the thing would actually work.

So that's where we are. Number one: Obamacare is helping millions of people right now. The uninsured rate has never been lower. It's helping

FOLLOWING THE June 28, 2012 Supreme Court Ruling upholding the ACA, the *Iowa City Press-Citizen* took a muted wait-and-see approach. As seen in the table above, a review of stock prices for the six largest U.S. health-care insurance companies saw their share price increase by a multiple of 3 to 5 times over their January 20, 2009 price to the day's price on January 20, 2017.

More than 22 million Americans previously uninsured or uninsurable benefitted from the ACA, in addition to the health-insurance industry.

everybody who already has health insurance, because it makes their policies better. Number two: there are still too many hardworking people who are not being reached by the law. Number three: if we tweak the program to reach those people who are not currently benefitting from the law, it will be good for them, and it will be good for the country. Number four: if we repeal this law wholesale, that will hurt the people who don't have coverage right now. It will hurt the 20 million who are already getting help through the law. And it will hurt the country as a whole.

So this should be an easy choice. All it requires is putting aside ideology and, in good faith, trying to implement the law of the land. And what we've learned, by the way, is that when governors and state legislators expand Medicaid for their citizens, and they hold insurance companies accountable, and they're honest with uninsured people about their options, and they're working with us on outreach, then the marketplace works the way it's supposed to. And when they don't, the marketplaces tend to have more problems. And that shouldn't be surprising. If state leaders purposely try to make something not work, then it's not going to run as smoothly as if they were trying to make it work. Common sense. You don't even have to go to Miami-Dade to figure that out.

The point is, now is not the time to move backward on health-care reform. Now is the time to move forward. The problems that may have arisen from the ACA is not because government is too involved in the process. The problem is that we have not reached everybody and pulled them in. Think about it. When one of these companies comes out with a new smartphone and it has a few bugs, what do they do? They fix it. They upgrade—unless it catches fire, and then they pull it off the market. But you don't go back to using a rotary phone. You don't say, "well, we're repealing smartphones—we're just going to do the dial-up thing." That's not what you do.

"All the progress that we've made in controlling costs and improving how health care is delivered, progress that's helped hold growth in the price of health care to the slowest rate in 50 years—all that goes away. That's what 'repeal' means."

Well, the same basic principle applies here. We're not going to go back to discriminating against Americans with preexisting conditions. We're not going to go back to a time when people's coverage was dropped when they got sick. We're not going to go back to a situation where we're reinstating lifetime limits in the fine print so that you think you have insurance, and then you get really sick or you kid gets really sick, and you hit the limit that the insurance company set, and next thing you know they're not covering you anymore, and you got to figure out how you come up with another $100,000 or $200,000 to make sure that your child lives. We're not going to go back to that.

I hear Republicans in Congress object, and they'll say, "no, no, no, no, we'll keep those parts of Obamacare that are popular; we'll just repeal everything else." Well, it turns out that the sum of those parts that are popular in Obamacare *is* Obamacare. It's just people don't always know it. And repealing it would make the majority of Americans worse off when it comes to health care.

And as I said, part of this is, you know, health care is complicated. Think about this speech—it's been pretty long, and you're thinking, "wow, I just want to take a picture with the president or something." So it's hard to get people focused on the facts. And even reporters who have covered this stuff—and they do a good job; they're trying to follow all the debate. But a lot of times they just report, "Premium increases." And everybody thinks, "wow, my insurance rates are going up, it must be Obama's fault"— even though you don't get health insurance through Obamacare, you get it through your job, and even though your increases have gone up a lot slower. Or suddenly you're paying a bigger copay, and, "ah, thanks, Obama." Well, no, I had nothing to do with that.

So part of it is this is complicated, the way it gets reported. There's a lot of hysteria around anything that happens. And what we need to do is focus on this specific problem—how do we make sure that more people are getting coverage, and folks who aren't getting tax credits or Medicaid, how do we help them? How do we reach them? And we can do it.

U.S. NEWSPAPERS reacted with headlines generally reflecting their political persuasion. While most chose to laud the Supreme Court decision, some saw it as looming question mark.

Instead of repealing the law, I believe the next president and the next Congress should take what we've learned over the past six years and, in a serious way, analyze it, figure out what it is that needs to get done, and make the Affordable Care Act better and cover even more people. But understand, no president can do it alone. We will need Republicans in Congress and in state governments to act responsibly and put politics aside. Because I want to remind you, a lot of the Affordable Care Act is built on Republican ideas.

In fact, Bernie Sanders is still mad at me because we didn't get single-payer passed. Now, we couldn't get single-payer passed, and I wanted to make sure that we helped as many people as possible, given the political constraints. And so we adopted a system that Republicans should like; it's based on a competitive, market-based system in which people have a responsibility for themselves to buy insurance.

And maybe now that I'm leaving office, maybe Republicans can stop with the 60-something repeal votes they've taken and stop pretending that they have a serious alternative and stop pretending that all the terrible things they said would happen have actually happened, when they have not, and just work with the next president to smooth out the kinks. Because it turns out, no major social innovation in America has ever worked perfectly at the start. Social Security didn't. Its benefits were stingy at first. It left out a whole lot of Americans. The same was true for Medicare. The same was true for Medicaid. The same was true for the prescription drug law. But what happened was, each year, people of goodwill from both parties tried to make it better. And that's what we need to do right now.

And I promise, if Republicans have good ideas to provide more coverage for folks like Amanda, I will be all for it. I don't care whose idea it is, I just want it to work. They can even change the name of the law to ReaganCare. Or they can call it PaulRyanCare. I don't care about credit, I just want it to work because I care about the American people and making sure they've got health insurance.

But that brings me to my final point: and that is change does not typically come from the top down, it always comes from the bottom up. The [ACA] was passed because the American people mobilized, not just to get me elected, but to keep the pressure on me to actually do something about health care and to put pressure on members of Congress to do something about it. And that's how change happens in America. It doesn't happen on its own, it doesn't happen from on high. It happens from the bottom up. And breaking gridlock will come only when the American people demand it.

So that's why I'm here. Only you can break this stalemate, by educating the public on the benefits of the Affordable Care Act, and then pressing your elected officials to do the right thing and supporting elected officials who are doing the right things. And this is one of the reasons why I'm so proud of what Miami-Dade College is doing, because it's making sure that students and faculty and people throughout this community know about the law, know about how to sign up for health care, and then actually helps people sign up. And I'm incredibly proud of the leadership Joe Peña and the entire team in encouraging people to sign up. . . .

"And I promise, if Republicans have good ideas to provide more coverage. . . . I will be all for it. I don't care whose idea it is, I just want it to work. They can even change the name. . . .I don't care about credit, I just want it to work because I care about the American people."

Joe says he doesn't have a conversation without making sure people know how to get covered. The more young and healthy people like you who do the smart thing and sign up, the better it's going to work for everybody. And the good news is, in a few days, you can do just that because . . . open enrollment begins on November 1. You just need to go to HealthCare.gov.

And campuses will be competing to come up with the most creative ways to reach people and get them signed up—and I'm pretty sure that Miami-Dade can set the standard for the rest of the country. 'Cause that's how you do. That's how you do.

So much has changed since I campaigned here in Miami eight Octobers ago. But one thing has not: this is more than just about health care. It's about the character of our country. It's about whether we look out for one another. It's about whether the wealthiest nation on earth is going to make sure that nobody suffers. Nobody loses everything they have saved, everything they have worked for because they're sick. You stood up for the idea that no American should have to go without the health care they need.

And it's still true today. And we've proven together that people who love this country can change it—20 million people out there will testify. I get letters every day just saying thank you because it's made a difference in their lives. And what was true then is true now. We still need you. Our work to expand opportunity to all and make our union more perfect is never finished—but the more we work, and organize, and advocate, and fight, the closer we get.

So I hope you are going to be busy this November signing folks up. But more importantly, I hope, for all the young people here, you never stop working for a better America. And even though I won't be president, I'll keep working right alongside you.

Thank you, everybody. God bless you. God bless America. Thank you. ★

WE DID IT! In the Situation Room of the White House, an excited Hillary Clinton congratulates President Obama on the House vote to pass health-care reform, March 22, 2010.

LAURIE GARRETT

Laurie Garrett is a Pulitzer Prize-winning author and a Senior Fellow for Global Health at the Council on Foreign Relations.

In addition to saving the world economy from the 2008 banking meltdown, the lynchpin of Barack Obama's presidency was healthcare: both domestic and foreign. Within weeks of taking office, the new president faced an outbreak of influenza that surfaced in Mexico City, filling hospitals there and spreading via students returning from Mexican vacations throughout the New York City school system. By late spring, cases of the new flu had emerged in all 50 states. But Obama's top health posts weren't yet filled, including the cabinet-level Secretary of Health and Human Services, and none of his security advisors had epidemic experience.

The 2009 H1N1 flu went global, and, despite urgent appeals from the White House, drug companies were unable to manufacture vaccines for use in most of the world— including the U.S.—until

outbreaks had come and gone.

While the White House struggled with Congress over "Obamacare," outbreaks kept emerging, revealing holes in the global and national disease safety nets. In 2012, Middle East Respiratory Syndrome, or MERS, arose in Saudi Arabia and continues to spread today, killing 42 percent of people it infects.

A year later, a highly virulent new influenza, H7N9, spread from birds to people across China, threatening a flu pandemic far worse than the 2009 one. Two forms of mutant super-bugs that infect bacteria, making them antibiotic-resistant, arose from Asia in 2011 and 2016, swiftly spreading into U.S. hospitals, where they rendered routine bacterial infections life-threatening. In 2014, the dreaded Ebola virus spread from wild bats in the Guinea Forest of West Africa across the nations of Liberia, Guinea, and Sierra Leone, prompting a global state of emergency. Distressed by a slow and ineffectual response from the World Health Organization, Obama ordered a massive U.S. effort to stop the

epidemic, including the first historic deployment of U.S. combat-ready troops for disease control.

President Obama and German Chancellor Angela Merkel felt the world needed to learn from the Ebola failures, building serious surveillance and response networks that reached into the the poorest nations on the planet. They created the Global Health Security Agenda (GHSA), deploying scientists to train counterparts, set up laboratories, and create outbreak rapid-response teams. By the end of 2016, fueled by $1 billion from the U.S., 50 nations were members of the GHSA.

The mosquito-carried Zika virus burst from anonymity in 2015 to threaten thousands of babies across Latin America. As it grew evident that the virus infected the brains of developing fetuses, causing a horrible range of congenital defects, miscarriages, and stillbirths when it infected pregnant women, Obama called on Congress to appropriate $1.9 billion for emergency research, drug and vaccine development,

and public health responses to Zika. Congress balked for eight months, forcing health and science agencies across federal and state governments to rob their public health budgets to stave off the virus.

As Obama's presidency came to its close, the futures of Obamacare and America's disease-fighting capabilities were uncertain. On the one hand, more than 30 million Americans were receiving health financing under the ACA, and insurers could no longer deny payments for treatment of preexisting conditions, such as diabetes or hypertension. U.S. scientists and drug companies, working in an unprecedented collaboration with colleagues from all over the world, developed a vaccine for Ebola that proved 100 percent effective. The enormous President's Emergency Plan for AIDS Relief initiated by President George W. Bush in 2003 was expanded under Obama, providing lifesaving medicine to some 12 million people infected with HIV, mostly in Africa, in 2016.

Measles—eliminated from the U.S. in 2000—reemerged

in 2015 out of a cluster of unvaccinated children visiting Disneyland in California, swiftly spreading across the U.S., Mexico, and Canada. Along with whooping cough and mumps outbreaks, the measles clusters revealed that many Americans were no longer vaccinating their children. Incredibly, as Obama stepped down, the Republican Congressional leadership and newly elected president vowed to destroy the ACA and greatly reduce the other health programs for poor and elderly Americans, including Medicaid and Medicare.

Above:

AMBER BRANTLY—whose husband, Dr. Kent Brantly, was the first American to contract Ebola—listens as President Obama delivers remarks at an event at the White House on October 29, 2014, with American health-care workers fighting the disease. Dr. Brantly contracted the Ebola virus while treating patients in West Africa and was subsequently cured. To Mrs. Brantly's left is Dr. Anthony Fauci, head of the National Institutes of Health.

ON THE
DISCLOSE ACT

July 26, 2010 | ROSE GARDEN, THE WHITE HOUSE
[ABRIDGED EXCERPT]

BECAUSE OF THE Supreme Court's decision earlier this year in the *Citizens United* case, big corporations, even foreign-controlled ones, are now allowed to spend unlimited amounts of money on American elections.

They can buy millions of dollars worth of TV ads—and worst of all, they don't even have to reveal who's actually paying for the ads. Instead, a group can hide behind a name like "Citizens for a Better Future," even if a more accurate name would be "Companies for Weaker Oversight." These shadow groups are already forming and building war chests of tens of millions of dollars to influence the fall elections.

U.S. SENATORS John McCain (R-AZ), left, and Russ Feingold (D-WI) at the Supreme Court on January 21, 2010, following arguments in *Citizens United v. Federal Election Commission*, a challenge to the campaign finance reform law the two authored. The court ruled that the law's ban on corporate expenditures was unconstitutional.

Now, imagine the power this will give special interests over politicians. Corporate lobbyists will be able to tell members of Congress if they don't vote the right way, they will face an onslaught of negative ads in their next campaign. And all too often, no one will actually know who's really behind those ads.

So the House has already passed a bipartisan bill that would change all this before the next election. The DISCLOSE Act would simply require corporate political advertisers to reveal who's funding their activities. So when special interests take to the airwaves, whoever is running and funding the ad would have to appear in the advertisement and claim responsibility for it—like a company's CEO or the organization's biggest contributor. And foreign-controlled corporations and entities would be restricted from spending money to influence American elections—just as they were in the past.

And you'd think that reducing corporate and even foreign influence over our elections would not be a partisan issue. But of course, this is Washington in 2010. And the Republican leadership in the Senate is once again using every tactic and every maneuver they can to prevent the DISCLOSE Act from even coming up for an up-or-down vote. Just like they did with unemployment insurance for Americans who'd lost their jobs in this recession. Just like they're doing by blocking tax credits and lending assistance for small-business owners. On issue after issue, we are trying to move America forward, and they keep on trying to take us back.

At a time of such challenge for America, we can't afford these political games. Millions of Americans are struggling to get by, and their voices shouldn't be drowned out by millions of dollars in secret, special interest advertising. The American people's voices should be heard.

A vote to oppose these reforms is nothing less than a vote to allow corporate and special-interest takeovers of our elections. It is damaging to our democracy. It is precisely what led a Republican president named Theodore Roosevelt to tackle this issue a century ago. ★

PRESIDENT OBAMA MAKES a statement on the Senate campaign finance reform vote to the press in the Rose Garden of the White House, July 26, 2010.

ON MARRIAGE EQUALITY

July 26, 2015 | ROSE GARDEN, THE WHITE HOUSE

GOOD MORNING. Our nation was founded on a bedrock principle that we are all created equal. The project of each generation is to bridge the meaning of those founding words with the realities of changing times—a never-ending quest to ensure those words ring true for every single American. Progress on this journey often comes in small increments, sometimes two steps forward, one step back, propelled by the persistent effort of dedicated citizens. And then sometimes, there are days like this when that slow, steady effort is rewarded with justice that arrives like a thunderbolt.

THE WHITE HOUSE is bathed in the symbolic rainbow of light celebrating the passage of the Defense of Marriage Act earlier in the day by the Supreme Court, June 26, 2015.

This morning, the Supreme Court recognized that the Constitution guarantees marriage equality. In doing so, they've reaffirmed that all Americans are entitled to the equal protection of the law. That all people should be treated equally, regardless of who they are or who they love.

This decision will end the patchwork system we currently have. It will end the uncertainty hundreds of thousands of same-sex couples face from not knowing whether their marriage, legitimate in the eyes of one state, will remain if they decide to move [to] or even visit another. This ruling will strengthen all of our communities by offering to all loving same-sex couples the dignity of marriage across this great land.

In my second inaugural address, I said that if we are truly created equal, then surely the love we commit to one another must be equal as well. It is gratifying to see that principle enshrined into law by this decision.

This ruling is a victory for Jim Obergefell and the other plaintiffs in the case. It's a victory for gay and lesbian couples who have fought so long for their basic civil rights. It's a victory for their children, whose families will now be recognized as equal to any other. It's a victory for the allies and friends and supporters who spent years, even decades, working and praying for change to come.

And this ruling is a victory for America. This decision affirms what millions of Americans already believe in their hearts: when all Americans are treated as equal we are all more free.

My administration has been guided by that idea. It's why we stopped defending the so-called Defense of Marriage Act and why we were pleased when the Court finally struck down a central provision of that discriminatory law. It's why we ended "Don't Ask, Don't Tell." From extending full marital benefits to federal employees and their spouses to expanding hospital visitation rights for LGBT patients and their loved ones, we've made real progress in advancing equality for LGBT Americans in ways that were unimaginable not too long ago.

I know change for many of our LGBT brothers and sisters must have seemed so slow for so long. But compared to so many other issues, America's shift has been so quick. I know that Americans of goodwill continue to hold a wide range of views on this issue. Opposition in some cases has been based on sincere and deeply held beliefs. All of us who welcome today's news should be mindful of that fact; recognize different viewpoints; revere our deep commitment to religious freedom.

But today should also give us hope that on the many issues with which we grapple, often painfully, real change is possible. Shifts in hearts and minds is possible. And those who have come so far on their journey to equality have a responsibility to reach

President Obama ✔
@POTUS

Follow

Today is a big step in our march toward equality. Gay and lesbian couples now have the right to marry, just like anyone else. #LoveWins

10:10 AM - 26 Jun 2015

↩ ⇄ 426,086   ♥ 424,599

"I know that Americans of goodwill continue to hold a wide range of views on this issue. Opposition in some cases has been based on sincere and deeply held beliefs. All of us who welcome today's news should be mindful of that fact; recognize different viewpoints; revere our deep commitment to religious freedom."

REBECCA GITLITZ *and* SAMANTHA RAPOPORT

Rebecca Gitlitz *(right) and* Samantha Rapoport *celebrate their marriage in Hudson, New York on November 5, 2016. Rebecca is a two-time Emmy Award-winning producer, and Samantha is a sports industry executive.*

No phone alert ever received was more numbing or body–chemistry altering than the one announcing the 5–4 Supreme Court ruling on Friday, June 26, 2015.

Across the country, from San Francisco City Hall to the Empire State Building to the White House and to our Brooklyn apartment, this decision was celebrated with the illumination of millions of lights in the colors of the rainbow: a symbol of the spectrum of liberties that were about to be bestowed upon us as a couple and upon our tight-knit community.

Though the lighting was eventually removed and the nationwide screams and cries of elation settled, this revolution sounded nothing like a whisper. The ruling indelibly changed our lives and the lives of hundreds of thousands of Americans. It finally granted us the right for which we shouldn't have had to fight this hard—for the government to equate our love to theirs, to marry the love of our lives, to have a legitimized future with those we cherish most; equality. The word "equal" means "the same." Now, because of one person, America uses the same word—married.

After the ruling, President Barack Obama called Jim Obergefell, the lead plaintiff in the case, offering, "I just wanted to say congratulations— your leadership on this has changed the country." It feels as though only President Obama would have approached this conversation in such a humbled way, not for a moment acting self-congratulatory even though it was his unparalleled and first-of-its-kind leadership that made the ruling a possibility.

Though President Obama may have taken no credit for the ruling in that conversation, our community has never doubted his influence. So thank you, President Obama, for standing up to injustice, for being the first sitting president to support marriage equality and say the words "gay, lesbian, and transgender" out loud, for making sure our unborn children never have to wonder why their moms aren't legally married, for allowing us to gain citizenship through marriage, for CHANGE, for HOPE, and mostly for the most valuable gift you could ever leave behind as you walk away: our marriage.

———

Author's Note: Rabbi Zoe B. Zak from Temple Israel of Catskill, New York, pronounces Samantha and Rebecca a legally married couple in the State of New York. As Rebecca's proud stepfather, it was a blessing to be there and to take this photo.

back and help others join them. Because, for all our differences, we are one people, stronger together than we could ever be alone. That's always been our story.

We are big and vast and diverse; a nation of people with different backgrounds and beliefs, different experiences and stories, but bound by our shared ideal that no matter who you are or what you look like, how you started off, or how and who you love, America is a place where you can write your own destiny. We are a people who believe that every single child is entitled to life and liberty and the pursuit of happiness.

There's so much more work to be done to extend the full promise of America to every American. But today, we can say in no uncertain terms that we've made our union a little more perfect.

That's the consequence of a decision from the Supreme Court, but, more importantly, it is a consequence of the countless small acts of courage of millions of people across decades who stood up, who came out, who talked to parents—parents who loved their children no matter what. Folks who were willing to endure bullying and taunts, and stayed strong, and came to believe in themselves and who they were, and slowly made an entire country realize that love is love.

What an extraordinary achievement. What a vindication of the belief that ordinary people can do extraordinary things. What a reminder of what Bobby Kennedy once said about how small actions can be like pebbles being thrown into a still lake, and ripples of hope cascade outwards and change the world.

Those countless, often anonymous heroes—they deserve our thanks. They should be very proud. America should be very proud. Thanks you. ★

VICE PRESIDENT BIDEN takes a selfie with guests during a reception to observe LGBT Pride Month in the East Room of the White House, June 24, 2015.

NBC NEWS SPECIAL REPORT
PRES. OBAMA ANNOUNCES OSAMA BIN LADEN KILLED

ON OSAMA BIN LADEN

Announced May 3, 2011, 11:35 P.M. EDT | THE WHITE HOUSE

GOOD EVENING. Tonight, I can report to the American people and to the world that the United States has conducted an operation that killed Osama bin Laden, the leader of al-Qaeda and a terrorist who's responsible for the murder of thousands of innocent men, women, and children.

It was nearly ten years ago that a bright September day was darkened by the worst attack on the American people in our history. The images of 9/11 are seared into our national memory—hijacked planes cutting through a cloudless September sky; the Twin Towers collapsing to the ground; black smoke billowing up from the Pentagon; the wreckage of Flight 93 in Shanksville, Pennsylvania, where the actions of heroic citizens saved even more heartbreak and destruction.

PRESIDENT OBAMA ANNOUNCES the death of Osama bin Laden live on television from the East Room of the White House.

And yet we know that the worst images are those that were unseen to the world. The empty seat at the dinner table. Children who were forced to grow up without their mother or their father. Parents who would never know the feeling of their child's embrace. Nearly 3,000 citizens taken from us, leaving a gaping hole in our hearts.

On September 11, 2001, in our time of grief, the American people came together. We offered our neighbors a hand, and we offered the wounded our blood. We reaffirmed our ties to each other and our love of community and country. On that day, no matter where we came from, what God we prayed to, or what race or ethnicity we were, we were united as one American family.

We were also united in our resolve to protect our nation and to bring those who committed this vicious attack to justice. We quickly learned that the 9/11 attacks were carried out by al-Qaeda—an organization headed by Osama bin Laden, which had openly declared war on the United States and was committed to killing innocents in our country and around the globe. And so we went to war against al-Qaeda to protect our citizens, our friends, and our allies.

Over the last ten years, thanks to the tireless and heroic work of our military and our counterterrorism professionals, we've made great strides in that effort. We've disrupted terrorist attacks and strengthened our homeland defense. In Afghanistan, we removed the Taliban government, which had given bin Laden and al-Qaeda safe haven and support. And around the globe, we worked with our friends and allies to capture or kill scores of al-Qaeda terrorists, including several who were a part of the 9/11 plot.

Yet Osama bin Laden avoided capture and escaped across the Afghan border into Pakistan. Meanwhile, al-Qaeda continued to operate from along that border and operate through its affiliates across the world.

And so shortly after taking office, I directed Leon Panetta, the director of the CIA, to make the killing or capture of bin Laden the top priority of our war against al-Qaeda even as we continued our broader efforts to disrupt, dismantle, and defeat his network.

Then, last August, after years of painstaking work by our intelligence community, I was briefed on a possible lead to bin Laden. It was far from certain, and it took many months to run this thread to ground. I met repeatedly with my national security team as we developed more information about the possibility that we had located bin Laden hiding within a compound deep inside Pakistan. And finally, last week, I determined that we had enough intelligence to take action and authorized an operation to get Osama bin Laden and bring him to justice.

Today, at my direction, the United States launched a targeted operation against that compound in Abbottabad, Pakistan. A small team of Americans carried out the operation with extraordinary courage and capability. No Americans were harmed. They took care to avoid civilian casualties. After a firefight, they killed Osama bin Laden and took custody of his body.

"On September 11, 2001, in our time of grief, the American people came together. We offered our neighbors a hand, and we offered the wounded our blood. . . . On that day, no matter where we came from, what God we prayed to, or what race or ethnicity we were, we were united as one American family."

THE TENSION is palpable in the Situation Room as the president and members of the National Security team anxiously follow live updates on the mission against Osama bin Laden, May 1, 2011. This is perhaps the most iconic picture taken during the Obama years.

For over two decades, bin Laden has been al-Qaeda's leader and symbol and has continued to plot attacks against our country and our friends and allies. The death of bin Laden marks the most significant achievement to date in our nation's effort to defeat al-Qaeda. Yet his death does not mark the end of our effort. There's no doubt that al-Qaeda will continue to pursue attacks against us. We must—and we will—remain vigilant at home and abroad.

As we do, we must also reaffirm that the United States is not—and never will be—at war with Islam. I've made clear, just as President Bush did shortly after 9/11, that our war is not against Islam. Bin Laden was not a Muslim leader; he was a mass murderer of Muslims. Indeed, al-Qaeda has slaughtered scores of Muslims in many countries, including our own. So his demise should be welcomed by all who believe in peace and human dignity.

Over the years, I've repeatedly made clear that we would take action within Pakistan if we knew where bin Laden was. That is what we've done. But it's important to note that our counterterrorism cooperation with Pakistan helped lead us to bin Laden and the compound where he was hiding. Indeed, bin Laden had declared war against Pakistan as well and ordered attacks against the Pakistani people.

Tonight, I called President Zardari, and my team has also spoken with their Pakistani counterparts. They agree that this is a good and historic day for both of our

THE SUCCESSFUL ELIMINATION of Osama Bin Laden was almost certainly the second biggest news event of the twenty-first century. Ironically, it served to give some degree of closure to what was, regrettably, the biggest story—9/11.

DAILY NEWS

NEW YORK'S HOMETOWN NEWSPAPER

ROT IN HELL!

NINE PAGES OF COVERAGE INSIDE

Obama: U.S. team kills Bin Laden in firefight

SECTION NAME · 87

nations. And going forward, it is essential that Pakistan continue to join us in the fight against al-Qaeda and its affiliates.

The American people did not choose this fight. It came to our shores and started with the senseless slaughter of our citizens. After nearly ten years of service, struggle, and sacrifice, we know well the costs of war. These efforts weigh on me every time I, as commander in chief, have to sign a letter to a family that has lost a loved one or look into the eyes of a service member who's been gravely wounded.

So Americans understand the costs of war. Yet as a country, we will never tolerate our security being threatened, nor stand idly by when our people have been killed. We will be relentless in defense of our citizens and our friends and allies. We will be true to the values that make us who we are. And on nights like this one, we can say to those families who have lost loved ones to al-Qaeda's terror: justice has been done.

Tonight, we give thanks to the countless intelligence and counterterrorism professionals who've worked tirelessly to achieve this outcome. The American people do not see their work, nor know their names. But tonight, they feel the satisfaction of their work and the result of their pursuit of justice.

We give thanks for the men who carried out this operation, for they exemplify the professionalism, patriotism, and unparalleled courage of those who serve our country. And they are part of a generation that has borne the heaviest share of the burden since that September day.

Finally, let me say to the families who lost loved ones on 9/11 that we have never forgotten your loss, nor wavered in our commitment to see that we do whatever it takes to prevent another attack on our shores.

And tonight, let us think back to the sense of unity that prevailed on 9/11. I know that it has, at times, frayed. Yet today's achievement is a testament to the greatness of our country and the determination of the American people.

The cause of securing our country is not complete. But tonight, we are once again reminded that America can do whatever we set our mind to. That is the story of our history, whether it's the pursuit of prosperity for our people; or the struggle for equality for all our citizens; our commitment to stand up for our values abroad; and our sacrifices to make the world a safer place.

Let us remember that we can do these things not just because of wealth or power but because of who we are: one nation, under God, indivisible, with liberty and justice for all.

Thank you. May God bless you. And may God bless the United States of America. ★

> "The American people did not choose this fight. It came to our shores and started with the senseless slaughter of our citizens. After nearly ten years of service, struggle, and sacrifice, we know well the costs of war. These efforts weigh on me every time I, as commander in chief, have to sign a letter to a family that has lost a loved one or look into the eyes of a service member who's been gravely wounded."

AT THE TENTH-ANNIVERSARY ceremonies of 9/11, during the dedication of the National September 11 Memorial in New York, former president George W. Bush, Laura Bush, President Obama, and the First Lady listen to Peter Negron (on-screen), whose father was killed in the attacks, September 11, 2011.

Since the U.S. Constitution first defined the role of commander in chief in 1789, much has changed. The scale, ferocity, and unstructured global nature of the conflicts for which the U.S. armed forces are "called into service" today are very different to anything imagined by the Founding Fathers.

Where once there were colonial militiamen brandishing front-loading muskets and, later, the trench-bound "over the top" warfare of 100 years ago, there are now nuclear weapons and unmanned arial vehicles, or "drones," unleashing pinpoint attacks from the safety of a command center thousands of miles from the target.

If the weaponry has changed, so too has the very definition of "war." Not since 1941, when FDR declared war on Japan, has a commander in chief issued the declaration that "a state of war now exists" with another nation, in name at least. All of the other engagements since then—Korea, Vietnam, the Persian Gulf, Afghanistan, Iraq, and others—were not wars, being classified instead as "extended military engagements."

When the Second World War began in September 1939, FDR didn't involve the U.S. until the Japanese made the decision for him with the December 7, 1941, attack on Pearl Harbor.

Since then, just about every president has had his own foreign conflicts to confront. George H. W. Bush led the United States into the 1991 Gulf War with Iraq and then after the terror attacks of 9/11, George W. Bush put U.S. troops into Afghanistan and Iraq—where they remain to this day.

Coming into office, Obama inherited these two wars with some 200,000 U.S. "boots on the ground." While he had made the campaign promise to end both wars, exacerbated in part by the unheralded emergence of ISIS, it turned out to be a more daunting challenge than anticipated. As of the end of the Obama administration, however, the total U.S. troops deployed in Afghanistan and Iraq was approximately 15,000.

As historian Alfred McCoy wrote in the *Nation* on September 15, 2015: "Viewed historically, Obama has set out to correct past foreign policy excesses and disasters, largely the product of imperial overreach, that can be traced to several generations of American leaders bent on the exercise of unilateral power. Within the spectrum of American state power, he has slowly shifted from the coercion of war, occupation, torture, and other forms of unilateral military action toward the more cooperative realm of trade, diplomacy, and security—all in search of a new version of American supremacy." ★

Previous pages:
PRESIDENT OBAMA SPEAKS to cadets at the U.S. Military Academy at West Point, December 9, 2009.

Opposite:
A GRATEFUL SOLDIER hugs President Obama following his remarks at Bagram Air Base, Afghanistan, May 25, 2014.

"Like Eisenhower, this generation of men and women in uniform know all too well the wages of war, and that includes those of you here at West Point. Four of the service members who stood in the audience when I announced the surge of our forces in Afghanistan gave their lives in that effort. A lot more were wounded. I believe America's security demanded those deployments. But I am haunted by those deaths, I am haunted by those wounds, and I would betray my duty to you and to the country we love if I ever sent you into harm's way simply because I saw a problem somewhere in the world that needed to be fixed, or because I was worried about critics who think military intervention is the only way for America to avoid looking weak."

—BARACK OBAMA, U.S. Military Academy,

PRESIDENT OBAMA AND Vice President Biden (not pictured) meet with combatant commanders and other military leaders in the Cabinet Room of the White House, December 2, 2014.

VETERANS

DESPITE PASSING THE July 2014 Veterans Affairs Reform Bill committing $16.3 billion to overhaul the Veterans Administration, President Obama is the first to admit that efforts to significantly improve the VA's service levels are still very much a "work in progress." On August 1, 2016, speaking at the 95th National Convention of Disabled American Veterans, he said: "America's commitment to our veterans is not just lines in a budget. And it can't be about politics. It's not even really about policy. Our commitment to our veterans is a sacred covenant. And I don't use those words lightly. It is sacred because there's no more solemn request than to ask someone to risk their life, to be ready to give their life on our behalf. It's a [sacred] covenant because both sides have responsibilities. Those who put on the uniform, you took an oath to protect and defend us, while the rest of us—the citizens you kept safe—we pledged to take care of you and your families when you come home. . . .That's a solemn promise that we make to each other. And it is binding. And upholding it is a moral imperative." ★

Opposite, top: PRESIDENT OBAMA AND Brigadier General Eric Kurilla view pictures of fallen military personnel at Bagram Air Force Base, Afghanistan, May 25, 2014.

Opposite, bottom: THE AUDIENCE LISTENS intently as the president speaks to military personnel at the Pensacola Naval Air Station in Pensacola, Florida, June 15, 2010.

Above: WORLD WAR II Veteran Kenneth (Rock) Merritt chats with Obama on the presidential helicopter, Marine One, after they attended the 70th French American D-Day commemoration ceremony in Normandy, France, June 20, 2014.

THE PRESIDENT AND FIRST Lady board
Air Force One at Berlin Tegel Airport prior to
departing Germany, June 19, 2013.

HOME AND ABROAD

AFTER HIS INAUGURATION on January 20, 2009, President Obama wasted no time in taking his first official trip outside the country. A mere 29 days after taking office, he flew 450 miles to Ottawa to meet with Canadian Prime Minister Stephen Harper. Obama went on to make 21 trips abroad in his first year— more than any other president. In his eight years in office, he would visit 58 countries.

But flying around the world in a private-edition Boeing 747 (aka Air Force One), is only one part of the presidential day-to-day. The often seemingly routine meeting, greeting, and entertaining of heads of state, royalty, religious leaders, and the occasional autocrat is all part of the job description for "Leader of the Free World."

During his time in office, however, a number of President Obama's diary entries have been far from routine. Among these transcendent occasions were his visits to Cuba and Hiroshima, Japan. In March

2016, to mark the softening of relations between two nations only 90 miles apart, Obama became the first sitting U.S. president in almost 90 years to visit Cuba; he had previously shaken hands with Cuban president Raúl Castro at Nelson Mandela's 2013 funeral in South Africa.

Combined with the Cuban initiative, other firsts, such as the president's May 2016 wreath laying at the Hiroshima Peace Memorial (see page 107) and Japanese Prime Minister Shinzō Abe's 75th-anniversary visit to the USS *Arizona* Memorial at -Pearl Harbor (opposite), all serve to demonstrate a concerted effort to build bridges rather than walls. ★

Above: PRESIDENT OBAMA EXTENDS the "hand of friendship" to Cuban president Raúl Castro at the Palacio de la Revolución, Havana, Cuba, March 21, 2016.

Opposite: PRIME MINISTER SHINZŌ ABE of Japan and President Obama place wreaths at the USS *Arizona* Memorial at Pearl Harbor, Hawaii, December 27, 2016.

UNITED STATES NAVY

Column 1

A. C. FORTENBERRY — COX
G. P. FOWLER — Sc
L. G. FRANK — Sc
C. D. FREDERICK — EMc
T. A. FREE — MMc
W. T. FREE — Sc
J. E. FRENCH — LCDR
R. N. FRIZZELL — Sc
R. W. FULTON — AMSMTHc
F. F. FUNK — BMc
L. H. FUNK — Sc

R. A. GAGER — Sc
E. R. GARGARO — Sc
R. W. GARLINGTON — Sc
O. W. GARRETT — SFc
G. E. GARTIN — Sc
W. F. GAUDETTE — Sc
R. M. GAULTNEY — EMc
P. R. GAZECKI — ENS
K. E. GEBHARDT — Sc
K. F. GEER — Sc
M. F. GEISE — Fc
S. H. GEMIENHARDT, Jr. — MMc
R. GHOLSTON — Yc
B. E. GIBSON — Sc
K. A. GIESEN — Yc
R. E. GILL — Sc
M. J. GIOVENAZZO — WTc
R. GIVENS — Yc
A. GOBBIN — SCc
W. C. GOFF — Sc
E. GOMEZ, Jr. — Sc
L. GOOD
W. A. GOODWIN — Sc
P. C. GORDON, Jr. — Fc
E. W. GOSSELIN — ENS
J. A. A. GOSSELIN — RMc
H. L. GOULD — Sc
R. C. GOVE — Sc
R. E. GRANGER — Fc
L. E. GRANT — Yc
A. J. GRAY — Fc
L. M. GRAY — Sc
W. J. GRAY, Jr. — Sc
G. H. GREEN — Sc
C. G. GREENFIELD — Sc
R. O. GRIFFIN — EMc
R. A. GRIFFITHS — EMc
R. B. GRISSINGER — Sc
W. W. GROSNICKLE — EMc
M. H. GROSS — CSK
R. G. GRUNDSTROM — Sc
J. H. GURLEY — SKc

C. I. HAAS — MUSc
S. W. HADEN — COX
F. B. HAFFNER — Fc
R. W. HAINES — Sc
J. R. HALL — CBM
W. I. HALLORAN — ENS
C. J. HAMILTON — Sc
E. C. HAMILTON — Sc
W. H. HAMILTON — Sc
G. W. HAMMERUD — Sc
"J" "D" HAMPTON — Sc
T. "W" HAMPTON
W. L. HAMPTON — Sc
D. D. HAN...
C. B. HA...
H. R. HA...
E. J. HA...
C. E. H...
K. W. H...
K. H. H...
G. E. H...
H. D...
W. H...
N. B...
P. J. H...
A. HA...

J. W...
H. L. AVIN...
R. D. HAWKINS
J. D. HAYES
K. M. HAYES
C. J. HAYNES
W. HAYS
J. C. HAZDOVAC
F. HEAD
V. HEATER
A. C. HEATH
R. L. HEBEL
W. HECKEN...
J. L. HEDGER
P. HEDRICK

Column 2

L. S. HEELY — Fc
E. J. HEIDT — Fc
W. J. HEIDT — MMc
M. C. HELM — Sc
W. W. HENDERSON — Sc
F. HENDRIKSEN — Fc
J. J. HERRING — SMc
R. A. HERRIOTT, Jr. — Sc
D. M. HESS — FCc
A. J. HESSDORFER — MMc
R. A. HIBBARD — BKRc
A. L. HICKMAN — SMc
E. O. HICKS — GMc
R. D. HICKS — PTRc
B. T. HILL — AOMc
H. V. HILTON — EMc
F. W. HINDMAN — Sc
G. V. HODGES — Fc
L. J. HOELSCHER — HAc
C. H. HOLLAND, Jr. — Sc
P. Z. HOLLENBACH — Sc
R. HOLLIS — LTJG
G. S. HOLLOWELL — COX
L. D. HOLMES — Sc
H. V. HOMER — Sc
H. D. HOPKINS — Sc
M. F. HORN — Fc
H. H. HORRELL — SMc
J. W. HORROCKS — CGM
J. E. HOSLER — Sc
C. R. HOUSE — CWT
J. J. HOUSEL — SKc
E. HOWARD — Fc
R. G. HOWARD — GMc
D. R. HOWE — Sc
L. HOWELL — COX
H. HUBBARD, 2c — MATTc
C. F. HUFFMAN — Fc
B. T. HUGHES — MUSc
L. B. HUGHES, Jr. — Sc
J. C. HUGHEY — Sc
D. C. HUIE — HAc
R. F. HUNTER — Sc
H. L. HUNTINGTON — Fc
W. H. HURD — MATTc
W. R. HURLEY — MUSc
L. I. HUVAL — Sc
A. A. HUYS — Sc
M. H. HYDE — COX

J. CIAK — Yc
H. B. IBBOTSON — Fc
R. F. INGALLS — SCc
T. "A" INGALLS — SCc
D. A. INGRAHAM — FCc
O. A. ISHAM — CGM
L. J. ISOM — Sc
N. K. IVERSEN — Sc
C. A. IVEY, Jr. — Sc

D. P. JACKSON, Jr. — Sc
R. W. JACKSON — Sc
J. B. JAMES — Sc
...E. JANTE
...IANZ
...ASTRZEMSKI
...ANS
...RIES
...JENKINS
...SEN
...ANY

R. JOHNSON
R. JOHNSON
S. C. JOHNSON — Sc
S. C. HUNTINGTON
B. S. JOLLEY — GMc
D. P. JONES — Sc
E. E. JONES — Sc
F. B. JONES — Sc
H. C. JONES — CWT
H. JONES, Jr. — CMc
H. J. JONES — Fc
H. L. JONES — GMc
L. JONES — Sc

Column 3

T. R. JONES — ENS
W. A. JONES — Yc
W. W. JONES — Sc
W. W. JONES — Sc
C. W. JOYCE — Fc
A. J. JUDD — COX

H. L. KAGARICE — CSK
R. O. KAISER — Sc
E. L. KATT — Sc
P. D. KELLER — MLDRc
J. D. KELLEY — SFc
W. L. KELLOGG — Fc
R. L. KELLY — CEM
D. L. KENISTON — Sc
K. H. KENISTON — Fc
K. F. KENNARD — GMc
C. C. KENNINGTON — Sc
M. H. KENNINGTON — Sc
T. T. KENT, Jr. — Sc
I. C. KIDD — RADM
BATTLESHIP DIV. COMMANDER
R. W. KIEHN — MMc
C. E. KIESELBACH — CMc
G. B. KING — Sc
L. C. KING — Sc
L. M. KING — Fc
R. N. KING, Jr. — ENS
F. W. KINNEY — Sc
G. L. KINNEY — QMc
W. A. KIRCHHOFF — Sc
T. L. KIRKPATRICK — CAPT
E. KLANN — SCc
R. E. KLINE — GMc
F. L. KLOPP — GMc
R. W. KNIGHT — EMc
W. KNUBEL, Jr. — Sc
K. E. KOCH — Sc
C. D. KOENEKAMP — Fc
H. O. KOEPPE — SCc
B. KOLAJAJCK — Sc
A. J. KONNICK — CMc
J. A. KOSEC — BMc
R. KOVAR — Sc
J. D. KRAMB — MSMTHc
J. H. KRAMB — Sc
R. R. KRAMER — GMc
F. J. KRAUSE — Sc
M. S. KRISSMAN — Sc
R. W. KRUGER — QMc
A. L. KRUPPA — Yc
H. H. KUKUK — Sc
S. KULA — SCc
D. J. KUSIE — RMc

R. P. LADERACH — FCc
W. R. LA FRANCE — Sc
...LAKE, Jr. — PAYCLK
...KIN
...A MAR — FCc
...RAMB — CSF
...NDMAN
...RY, Jr. — BKRc
— COX

Column 4

J. W. LINCOLN — Fc
J. M. LINDSAY — SFc
G. E. LINTON — Fc
C. W. LIPKE — Fc
J. A. LIPPLE — SFc
D. E. LISENBY — Sc
R. E. LIVERS — Sc
W. N. LIVERS — Fc
D. A. LOCK — Sc
E. W. LOHMAN — Sc
F. S. LOMAX — ENS
M. LOMIBAO — OSc
B. F. LONG — CY
T. W. LOUNSBURY — Sc
C. B. LOUSTANAU — Sc
F. C. LOVELAND — Sc
N. J. LUCEY — Sc
J. E. LUNA — Sc
E. B. LUZIER — MMc
E. L. LYNCH — MUSc
J. R. LYNCH, Jr. — GMc
W. J. LYNCH, Jr. — Sc

R. D. MADDOX — CEM
A. J. MADRID — Sc
F. R. MAFNAS — MATTc
G. J. MAGEE — SKc
F. E. MALECKI — CY
J. S. MALINOWSKI — SMc
H. L. MALSON — SKc
E. P. MANION — Sc
A. C. MANLOVE — ELEC
W. E. MANN — GMc
L. MANNING — Sc
F. MANSKE — Yc
S. M. MARINICH — COX
E. H. MARIS — Sc
J. H. MARLING — Sc
U. H. MARLOW — COX
B. R. MARSH, Jr. — ENS
W. A. MARSH — Sc
T. D. MARSHALL — Sc
H. L. MARTIN — Yc
J. A. MARTIN — BMc
J. O. MARTIN — Sc
L. L. MARTIN — Fc
B. D. MASON — Sc
C. H. MASTEL — Sc
D. M. MASTERS — GMc
C. E. C. MASTERSON — PHMc
H. R. MATHEIN — BMKRc
C. H. MATHISON — Sc
V. M. MATNEY — Fc
J. D. MATTOX — AMc
L. E. MAY — SCc
G. F. MAYBEE — RMc
L. E. MAYFIELD — Fc
R. H. MAYO — EMc
W. McCARY — Sc
J. C. McCLAFFERTY — BMc
H. M. McCLUNG — ENS
L. J. McFADDIN, Jr. — Yc
J. O. McGLASSON — Sc
S. W. G. McGRADY — MATTc
F. R. McGUIRE — SKc
J. B. McHUGHES — CW...
H. G. McINTOSH — Sc
R. McKINNIE — Sc
M. M. McKOSKY — Fc
J. B. McPHERSON — Fc
L. MEANS — Sc
J. M. MEARES — Sc
J. A. MENE...

Column 5

J. MLINAR — COX
R. P. MOLPUS — CMSMTH
D. MONROE — MATTc
R. E. MONTGOMERY — Sc
R. E. MOODY — Fc
D. C. MOORE — Sc
F. K. MOORE — Sc
J. C. MOORE — SFc
W. S. MOORHOUSE — MUSc
R. L. MOORMAN — Sc
W. MORGAN — Sc
J. O. MORGAREIDGE — Fc
E. E. MORLEY — Fc
O. N. MORRIS — Sc
R. H. MORRISON — Sc
E. C. MORSE — Sc
F. J. MORSE — BMc
G. R. MORSE — Sc
N. R. MORSE — WTc
T. L. MOSS — MATTc
G. E. MOULTON — Fc
R. MUNCY — MMc
C. L. MURDOCK — WTc
M. E. MURDOCK — WTc
J. H. MURPHY — Sc
J. J. MURPHY — Sc
J. P. MURPHY — Fc
T. J. MURPHY, Jr. — SKc
J. G. MYERS — SKc

E. H. NAASZ — SFc
A. J. NADEL — MUSc
J. G. NATIONS — FCc
"J" "D" NAYLOR — SMc
T. D. NEAL — Sc
C. R. NECESSARY — Sc
P. NEIPP — Sc
G. NELSEN — SCc
H. C. NELSON — Sc
H. C. NELSON — BMc
L. A. NELSON — CTC
R. E. NELSON — Sc
A. R. NICHOLS — Fc
B. A. NICHOLS — Sc
C. L. NICHOLS — TCc
L. D. NICHOLS — Sc
G. E. NICHOLSON — EMc
H. G. NICHOLSON — Sc
T. J. NIDES — EMc
F. T. NIELSEN — CMc
R. H. NOONAN — Sc
T. L. NOWOSACKI — ENS
R. A. NUSSER — GMc
F. E. NYE — Sc

G. D. O'BRYAN — FCc
J. R. O'BRYAN — FCc
H. F. OCHOSKI — GMc
V. S. OFF — Sc
...OGLE
...ESBY — Sc
...ER — Sc
...ON — ENS
...ON — Sc
...ALL, Jr. — ENS

Column 6

W. H. PEAVEY — QMc
H. W. PECKHAM — Fc
M. V. PEERY — Sc
M. PELESCHAK — Sc
J. A. PELTIER — EMc
H. L. PENTON — Sc
G. E. PERKINS — Fc
A. H. PETERSON, Jr. — FCc
E. V. PETERSON — FCc
H. W. PETERSON — Fc
R. E. PETERSON — Sc
C. R. PETTIT — CRM
J. J. PETYAK — Sc
G. E. PHELPS — Sc
J. R. PHILBIN — Sc
H. L. PIKE — EMc
L. I. PIKE — Sc
A. W. PINKHAM — Sc
W. G. PITCHER — GMc
E. L. POOL — Sc
R. E. POOLE — Sc
D. A. POST — CMM
G. POVESKO — Sc
T. G. POWELL — Fc
W. H. PRESSON — Sc
A. E. PRICE — RMc
R. L. PRITCHETT, Jr. — Sc
E. L. PUCKETT — SKc
J. PUGH, Sr. — SFc
A. B. PUTNAM — SCc
E. PUZIO — Sc

M. J. QUARTO — Sc
J. S. QUINATA — MATTc

N. J. RADFORD — MUSc
A. S. RASMUSSEN — CMc
G. V. RASMUSSON — Fc
W. RATKOVICH — WTc
G. D. RAWHOUSER — Fc
C. J. RAWSON — BMc
H. J. RAY — BMc
C. REAVES — Sc
C. C. RECTOR — SKc
J. J. REECE — Sc
J. B. REED, Jr. — SKc
R. E. REED — Sc
P. J. REGISTER — LCDR
J. M. RESTIVO — Yc
E. A. REYNOLDS — Sc
J. F. REYNOLDS — Sc
B. R. RHODES — Fc
M. A. RHODES — Sc
W. A. RICE — Sc
C. E. RICH — Sc
C. R. RICHARD — Sc
W. J. RICHARDSON — COX
F. L. RICHISON — GMc
A. W. RICHTER — COX
G. A. RICO — Sc
F. RIGANTI — SFc
F. E. RIDDELL — Sc

Clockwise from top left:
QUEEN ELIZABETH II GREETS President Obama and the First Lady at Buckingham Palace, London, April 1, 2009; Obama welcomes His Holiness the Dalai Lama to the White House, June 15, 2016; Israeli president Shimon Peres meets with President Obama in the Oval Office, May 5, 2009; Obama and King Abdullah II of Jordan meet in the Oval Office for talks on ending the conflict in Syria and finding a solution for the refugee crisis, February 24, 2016.

AIR FORCE ONE

- In his two terms, Air Force One (AF1) has taken the president on 445 "missions."

- He has flown 2,799 hours and 6 minutes* on AF1—that's 116 days in the sky.

- AF1 has taken President Obama to 56 countries and 49 states—Maryland is the only state he missed.

- The ability to refuel in flight means AF1 has unlimited range and, in the event of an attack on the U.S., can function as a mobile command center.

- Onboard electronics are hardened to protect against an electromagnetic pulse, and the aircraft has advanced secure-communications equipment.

- The president and his companions enjoy 4,000 square feet of space on three levels; the president's suite features an office and conference room.

- There is a medical suite/operating room, and a doctor is permanently on board.

- Two galley kitchens can feed 100 people at a time. ★

*Travel + Leisure, January 11, 2017, "according to the pool report."

Above: IN HIS OFFICE aboard Air Force One during a flight to Riyadh, Saudi Arabia, on March 28, 2014, President Obama meets with, from left: Secretary of State John Kerry; National Security Advisor Susan E. Rice; Phil Gordon, White House Coordinator for the Middle East, North Africa, and the Gulf Region; and Ben Rhodes, Deputy National Security Advisor for Strategic Communications.

Opposite, clockwise from top left: THE PRESIDENT WALKS with Burmese activist Aung San Suu Kyi after a joint press conference in Yangon, Myanmar, November 2014; Obama walks with Kenyan president Uhuru Kenyatta at the State House in Nairobi, Kenya, July 25, 2015; Pope Francis and President Obama stroll through the Colonnade at the White House, September 23, 2015.

Clockwise from top left:
AN ENTHUSIASTIC CROWD engulfs the president following a speech in Prague, April 2009; Obama—the first U.S. president to visit Hiroshima—and Japanese prime minister Shinzō Abe talk after laying wreaths at the Peace Memorial Park in Hiroshima, May 27, 2016; Chinese president Xi Jinping views the Bliss Copy of the Gettysburg Address in the Lincoln Bedroom, September 25, 2015; the president—with Nobel Laureate and Holocaust survivor Elie Weisel, German chancellor Angela Merkel, and International Buchenwald Committee President Bertrand Herz—places a rose on a memorial at the site of the former Buchenwald concentration camp in Germany, June 5, 2009.

PRESIDENT VLADIMIR PUTIN of Russia and President Obama shake hands for the cameras before a tense bilateral meeting at the United Nations headquarters in New York, September 28, 2015.

Clockwise from this image:
ROBERT BYRD, 51 years a U.S. senator, is laid to rest at the State Capitol in Charleston, West Virginia, July 2, 2010; the president stands alongside Israeli prime minister Benjamin Netanyahu at the funeral of former Israeli president Shimon Peres, Jerusalem, September 30, 2016; as European leaders look on, President Obama speaks with U.S. veterans Ben Franklin and Clyde Combs (left) during the 65th anniversary of the D-Day invasion, Normandy, France, June 6, 2009.

THE WORST OF TIMES

Every eight-year period has its share of trials and tribulations, and the Obama years were no exception.

An ever-less-caring Mother Nature found more frequent ways to wreak havoc by way of earthquake, hurricane, typhoon, tornado, drought, and flood, and while the vast majority of scientists agree that humankind is at least partly responsible, some still doggedly choose to disagree.

According to the National Climatic Data Center, during the Obama years there were 77 major natural disasters that took 1,592 lives and did $300 billion in damage. Sometimes just showing up is what really matters, and Obama believed that being there in person, feeling the pain, dispensing hugs, and listening were paramount.

As devastating as nature can be, the insanity of man's inhumanity to man is even more tragic. With only 4.5 percent of the world's population, since 1966 the United States has had approximately 30 percent of the mass shootings. In Chicago alone during 2016 there were 4,368 shooting incidents and 763 deaths—a 58 percent increase on the prior year and more than Los Angeles and New York combined.

Following tragedies like the Sandy Hook Elementary School murder of 26 children and teachers—the deadliest shooting at a primary or secondary school in U.S. history—Obama repeatedly implored lawmakers to introduce more effective gun control measures. Sadly, his cries were consistently frustrated at every turn by an intransigent congress and the NRA's stranglehold on anything that might be cloaked as an attack on Second Amendment rights.

An increasing incidence of questionable shootings by law enforcement resulted in ever more tense relationships between the public and the police and gave birth to movements like Black Lives Matter. At yet another memorial service, this time on July 12, 2016, for the five police officers ambushed in Dallas, the president again found himself facing an audience of newly bereaved, aggrieved, and angry citizens. His speech highlighted his own frustration with the situation: "Faced with this violence, we wonder if the divides of race in America can ever be bridged. We wonder if an African American community that feels unfairly targeted by police, and police departments that feel unfairly maligned for doing their jobs, can ever understand each other's experience."

We all have to pray they can. ★

Previous pages:
PRESIDENT OBAMA IS moved to tears as he discusses the heartache caused by gun deaths during an announcement of new executive actions to try to reduce gun violence in the East Room of the White House, January 5, 2016.

Opposite:
THE PRESIDENT AND vice president place flowers on the makeshift memorial honoring the victims of the Pulse nightclub massacre at the Dr. Phillips Center for the Performing Arts in Orlando, Florida, June 16, 2016.

"Let the little children come to me, Jesus said, and do not hinder them . . . for to such belongs the Kingdom of Heaven.

CHARLOTTE.

DANIEL.

OLIVIA.

JOSEPHINE.

ANA.

DYLAN.

MADELEINE.

CATHERINE.

CHASE.

JESSE.

JAMES.

GRACE.

EMILIE.

JACK.

NOAH.

CAROLINE.

JESSICA.

BENJAMIN.

AVIELLE.

ALLISON.

God has called them all home."

—BARACK OBAMA at Sandy Hook interfaith prayer vigil, Newtown High School, Newtown, Connecticut, December 16, 2012

FOLLOWING THE FAILURE of the background-check bill in April 2013, President Obama spoke from the White House Rose Garden flanked by Congresswoman Gabrielle Giffords, who was wounded in a January 2011 Tuscon shooting, and parents of slain children at Newtown. "It came down to politics," the president said, and that "there are no coherent arguments for why we didn't do this. All in all, this was a pretty shameful day for Washington." Mark Barden, the father of one slain student, said "Our hearts are broken, our spirit is not."

June 12, 2016, Orlando Florida
49 DEAD, 53 INJURED

July 20, 2012, Aurora, Colorado
12 DEAD, 70 INJURED

October 1, 2015, Roseburg, Oregon
9 DEAD, 9 INJURED

27 DEAD, 2 INJURED

3 DEAD, 264 INJURED

9 DEAD, 1 INJURED

Obama offers 'love, prayers'

By JIM KUHNHENN, Associated Press

NEWTOWN — He spoke for a nation in sorrow, but the slaughter of all those little boys and girls left President Barack Obama, like so many others, reaching for words.

"I can only hope it brings some measure of comfort..."

See **PRESIDENT** Page A10

Inside: Norwalk holds a vigil in honor of those killed in Newtown..... Page A3

The Hour
thehour.com · The Independent Voice of the Community For 141 Years

REMEMBERING THE VICTIMS | The names and stories of the 27 who lost their lives.

Grace McDonnell, 7
Mary Sherlach, 56, school psychologist
Emilie Parker, 6
Lauren Rousseau, 30, teacher
Chase Kowalski, 7
Olivia Engel, 6

Jesse Lewis, 6

James Mattioli, 6
Caroline Previdi, 6
Arielle Richman, 6
Dylan Hockley, 6
Owen Hochsprung, 47, principal

Profiles continued on Page A6

TAUNTON DAILY GAZETTE
Serving Taunton, Raynham, Dighton, Berkley, Rehoboth and surrounding communities

TUESDAY APRIL 16, 2013
Volume 235, Number 106 · 75¢

A commitment to the community since 1848.

"Marathon Monday is usually one of the best days of the year in Boston. But it wasn't this Monday."
— Matt Dormody, Taunton native

'ABSOLUTE CHAOS'

PATRIOTS DAY VICTORY
Napoli gets walk-off double to lift Boston Red Sox over Tampa Bay Rays in three-game sweep. SPORTS, B1

STANDING THEIR GROUND

KITES IN FLIGHT

Boston rocked by explosions; Tauntonians recount tragedy

3 dead, over 130 injured in bombing

Sunday, June 21, 2015
The Post and Courier

IN REMEMBRANCE

Cynthia Hurd
54, a library manager whose life was dedicated to books, children and church

Susie Jackson
87, a mother figure to generations in her family and a renowned cook of collard greens

Ethel Lance
70, a church custodian who found strength in a gospel song to overcome life's challenges

DePayne Middleton Doctor
49, a minister whose angelic voice could heal troubled hearts

Clementa Pinckney
41, a pastor and state senator who lent his booming voice to the voiceless

Tywanza Sanders
26, a barber, poet and aspiring entrepreneur ready to take the world by storm

Daniel L. Simmons Sr.
74, a minister who served as a model of endurance and service to God

Sharonda Singleton
45, a pastor and coach who became her runners' biggest cheerleader, on and off the track

Myra Thompson
59, a builder of faith who worked to restore her beloved church's properties to their full glory

---

14 DEAD, 22 INJURED

5 DEAD, 11 INJURED

SERVING THE PUBLIC SINCE 1878 · WINNER OF 18 PULITZER PRIZES

ST. LOUIS POST-DISPATCH
THURSDAY · 12.03.2015 · $1.50

14 DIE IN ATTACK

'CAME PREPARED'
Attackers were armed with assault rifles and wearing masks and vests

AT LEAST 12 INJURED
Assailants opened fire in a San Bernardino, Calif., social services center

TWO SUSPECTS KILLED
Hours later, one man and one woman were killed after a high-speed chase

POTENTIAL MOTIVES
FBI is investigating workplace retaliation or perhaps terrorism

Community college enrollment plummets

NFL owners tell St. Louis to finalize stadium plan

Cards Keep Moss

Baden boosters see opportunity in buyouts

Longview News-Journal
LONGVIEW, TEXAS · **SUNDAY** July 10, 2016 · news-journal.com

POLICE SHOOTINGS

OUR BLACK & BLUE DIVIDE

In the wake of a week of violence, area law enforcement emphasizes building trust, while black East Texans voice concerns, apprehension

"I don't think you feel safe anywhere in America considering the things that have happened in the last few weeks and considering what's happened in this country." — RANDALL WEBSTER OF LONGVIEW, WHO IS BLACK

County sends 4 to Ohio, Philly
East Texans prepare for national GOP, Dem events

Report: Area rents rise slightly as income falls

BLACK EAST TEXANS
Some wary of traffic stops, armed or not

AREA POLICE
Goal better relationships, sense of safety

NEWSPAPER FRONT PAGES from across the country bear witness to the scourge of gun violence over a four-year period.

Note: Casualty statistics do not include perpetrators.

ON JUNE 21, 2016, concluding a moving speech on the need for the House to take action on gun violence before going on recess, Rep. John Lewis (D-GA) thundered, "We have lost hundreds and thousands of innocent people to gun violence. . . . And what has this body done, Mr. Speaker? Nothing. Not one thing." So began a dramatic 26-hour sit-in by Democrats on the floor of the House, shown here in a still image from C-SPAN video.

THE PRESIDENT CONSOLES a woman in
Joplin, Missouri, on May 29, 2011, a week after
the city was hit by a tornado that took 165 lives
and caused almost $3 billion in damages—the
worst to hit the nation since 1947.

NEW JERSEY GOVERNOR Chris Christie greets President Obama and FEMA Administrator Craig Fugate en route to the devastation of Superstorm Sandy, Atlantic City Airport, New Jersey, October 31, 2012.

Opposite top and bottom: SMASHED BOATS in a pile in a marina in Sayreville, New Jersey, destroyed by Sandy's wrath; Obama comforting residents of Joplin, Missouri, after a catastrophic tornado ravaged the city, May 2011.

SIR RICHARD BRANSON

Sir Richard Branson *is the founder of the Virgin Group, a tie-loathing adventurer, and a philanthropist who believes in turning ideas into reality.*

Over the years, I have met many heads of state—some, like Nelson Mandela, have left an indelible impression on me, while unfortunately several others left me more "de-pressed" than "im-pressed": I won't name names. President Obama however, is someone who has always managed to raise my spirits, even when he seems to have been under constant attack from all sides.

With about six months left in his second term, I was invited to the White House for a one-on-one lunch and chat in the Oval Office. The president opened the conversation by telling me that he always kept an eye on the various not-for-profit initiatives in which the Virgin Group is involved, such as climate change, conflict resolution, protecting the ocean, prison and drug reform, capital punishment, and, of course, inspiring young entrepreneurs. The conversation was such that it was quickly clear that he was indeed very much tuned into the same issues, and, to my delight, we seemed to be closely aligned on most of them.

We then went on to discuss another of my passions, kite-surfing, as well as personal challenges and even space travel—I felt he really wants to fly with Virgin Galactic, but we shall see. I was then surprised to be asked by the President of the United States about how I manage to maintain a healthy balance between work and play, something that I only then realized must be a huge challenge for anyone in his incredibly stressful position—especially with teenage daughters!

That same evening I was back at the White House to celebrate the president's 55th birthday. Assuming

(correctly) all the ladies would be dressed to the nines, I buckled and wore a suit but drew the line at wearing a tie. Then I saw Obama in jeans! Probably the first time in my life I have felt overdressed, and it was at the White House.

During his time in office, President Obama faced constant obstruction and harsh criticism but kept pushing forward. He showed great courage and determination in bringing the U.S. into the Paris Agreement to cut global emissions—an accord that, without America, simply will not work. The world now holds its breath to see if his good work will survive with the next administration.

One thing seems for sure: the Obamas will go on to do a great deal more good in the world in the coming years.

———

Above:
Sir Richard Branson at a luncheon with President Obama at the White House in December 2016.

Clockwise from top:
GREENHOUSE GASES HAVE created global health emergencies, and residents of Beijing are often forced to wear masks and use headlights in the daytime; Senator James Inhofe (R-OK) brings a snowball into the Senate chamber to support his claim that climate change is "the greatest hoax ever perpetrated on the American people," February 2015; Obama promotes renewable energy at a solar-energy field in Boulder City, Nevada, March 2012; Secretary of State John Kerry, with his granddaughter, signs the 2016 Paris Agreement for the United States—which led the effort—at the United Nations on Earth Day, April 22, 2016.

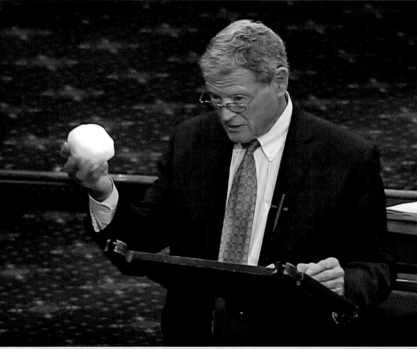

"I do think that part of what contributed to this [Flint water] crisis was a . . . corrosive attitude that exists in our politics and in too many levels of our government. And it's a mindset that believes that less government is the highest good no matter what. It's a mindset that says environmental rules designed to keep your water clean are optional, or not that important, or unnecessarily burden businesses or taxpayers. It's an ideology that undervalues the common good, says we're all on our own and what's in it for me? . . . And, as a consequence, you end up seeing an underinvestment in the things that we all share that make us safe, that make us whole, that give us the ability to pursue our own individual dreams. . . . Because what happens is it leads to systematic neglect. It leads to carelessness and callousness. It leads to a lot of hidden disasters that you don't always read about and aren't as flashy, but that over time diminish the life of a community and make it harder for our young people to succeed."

—BARACK OBAMA to the Flint,
Michigan community, May 4, 2016

Above and opposite: AFTER ADDRESSING A crowd of concerned residents at Flint Northwestern High School, President Obama takes a drink of filtered local water, Flint, Michigan, May 4, 2016.

"You know, when Trayvon Martin was first shot, I said that this could have been my son. Another way of saying that is Trayvon Martin could have been me 35 years ago. . . . I think it's important to recognize that the African American community is looking at this issue through a set of experiences and a history that doesn't go away."

—BARACK OBAMA on Trayvon Martin in the James S. Brady Press Briefing Room, the White House, July 19, 2013

Opposite:
DEMONSTRATORS OUTSIDE the Greater St. Mark Family Church in St. Louis on August 12, 2014, protesting the police shooting of Michael Brown, 18, three days earlier.

Clockwise from top: **Michael Brown** of Ferguson, Missouri; Tamir Rice of Cleveland, Ohio; Trayvon Martin of Miami Gardens, Florida; Philando Castile, of Saint Paul, Minnesota.

FOLLOWING THE DEATH of Trayvon Martin in 2013 and culminating in riots in Ferguson, Missouri, after the shooting death of Michael Brown, the Black Lives Matter movement gained new momentum with its protests to bring attention to the ways in which black lives are deprived of basic human rights and dignity.

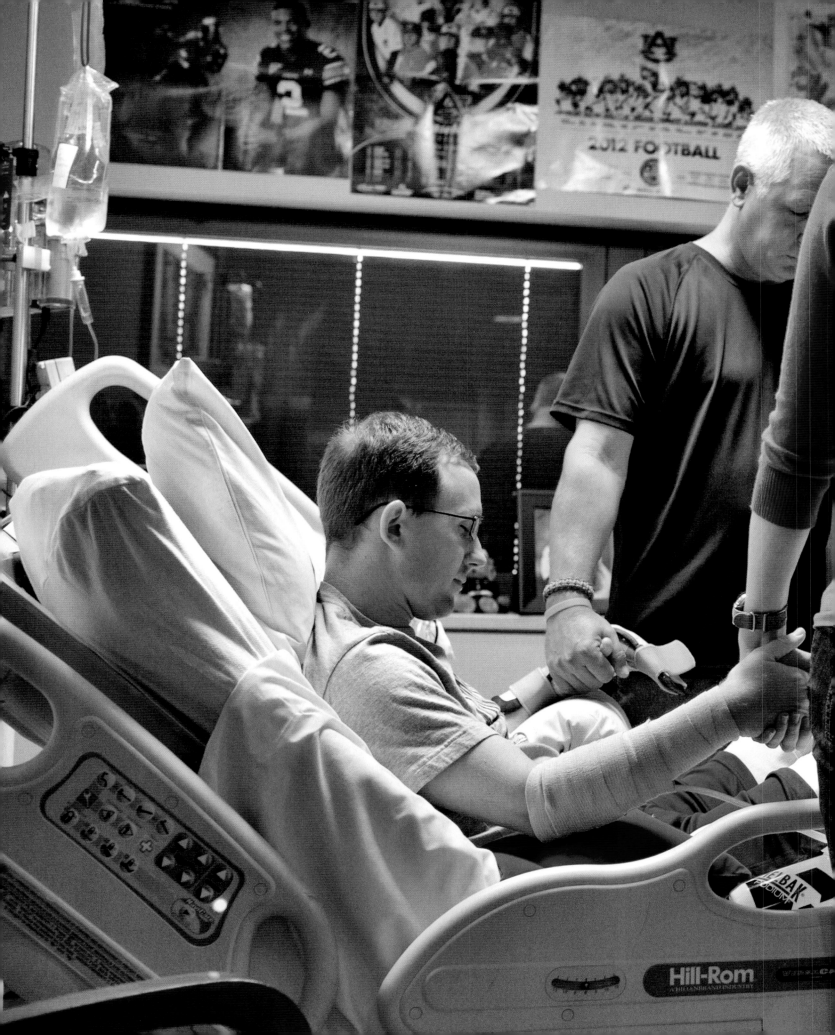

HONOR ROLL

Our heroes come home from the field of battle in many different ways. The lucky ones return to their families physically unscathed. Some return with life-altering injuries, while others battle the invisible but grievous wound of PTSD. The less fortunate return in flag-draped coffins. They are all heroes.

Created in 1862, the Medal of Honor—also known as the "Congressional Medal of Honor"—is the nation's highest military honor. Awarded by the president, the medal goes to Army, Navy, and Air Force personnel that have "distinguished themselves conspicuously by gallantry and intrepidity in combat with an enemy of the United States."

In March 2014, President Obama presented 24 Medals of Honor—all but three posthumously—in what was the largest group of honorees since World War II. What made this event truly historic was that most of the 24 were initially passed over because they were Hispanic, Jewish, or African American. Prompted by a law passed in 2002, intensive research by the Pentagon into possible past discrimination in Medal of Honor decision-making revealed that 19 men were denied the honor for racial and ethnic reasons.

President Obama commented, "This ceremony reminds us of one of the enduring qualities that makes America exceptional. No nation is perfect, but here in America, we confront our imperfections and face a sometimes painful past, including the truth that some of these soldiers fought and died for a country that did not always see them as equal."

Marveling at how these men have led their lives in the wake of such valor, the president went on to cite Vietnam veteran Jose Rodela. Formerly a Special Forces company commander, Rodela is now a 76-year-old retiree who frequently mows his neighbors' lawns. "Jose is such a humble guy that he did not even mention this ceremony to his neighbors, who I think would be pretty shocked to turn on the news tonight and see that the guy who cuts their lawn is getting the Medal of Honor." ★

Previous pages:
DURING A VISIT to Walter Reed National Military Medical Center in Bethesda, Maryland, President Obama prays with Spc. Josh Wetzel and his family, June 28, 2012. Spc. Wetzel of Glencoe, Alabama, lost both his legs to an IED bomb during a foot patrol in Afghanistan.

Opposite:
UNTIL THE OBAMA administration changed it, for almost two decades there was a Department of Defense press ban on showing the flag-draped coffins of returning heroes. This blinkered policy was rescinded in February 2009. The image here was taken in Kuwait in 2004.

HONORING THE MILITARY: President Obama applauds Medal of Honor recipient retired Army Capt. Florent Groberg after presenting the medal during a ceremony in the East Room of the White House. Groberg received the medal for actions during service in Afghanistan, where he tackled a suicide bomber, saving the lives of many and being severely injured in the process, November 12, 2015.

Above:

PRESIDENT OBAMA PRESENTS a posthumous Medal of Honor to Elsie Shemin-Roth and Ina Bass on June 2, 2015. Their father, Army Sergeant William Shemin, distinguished himself while serving in France during World War I. *Left:* The president applauds Medal of Honor recipients (l-r) Staff Sgt. Melvin Morris, Master Sgt. Jose Rodela (saluting), and Specialist Santiago Erevia for actions during the Vietnam War, during a ceremony in the White House on March 18, 2014.

Opposite:

THE PRESIDENT PRESENTS the Medal of Honor to Army Command Sgt. Major Bennie Adkins for acts of gallantry during the Vietnam War, September 15, 2014.

INDEPENDENCE DAY 2014. At the White House, Airman First Class Karen Mae Manalo joyously greets the president prior to a naturalization ceremony for active-duty members of the military.

MEDAL OF FREEDOM

THE PRESIDENTIAL MEDAL of Freedom is the highest civilian award in the U.S. It was re-crafted in 1963 by President John F. Kennedy, superseding the Medal of Freedom established by President Harry S. Truman in 1945 to honor civilian service during World War II.

The current medal is awarded by the president "for especially meritorious contribution to either the security or national interests of the United States, world peace, or cultural or other significant public or private endeavors." Or, as President Obama stated prior to the 2016 awards, "The Medal of Freedom is a tribute to the idea that all of us, no matter where we come from, have the opportunity to change this country for the better. From scientists, philanthropists, and public servants to activists, athletes, and artists, these 21 individuals have helped push America forward, inspiring millions of people around the world along the way."

Recipients of the Presidential Medal of Freedom are selected by the president or recommended to him by the Distinguished Civilian Service Awards Board. Awardees need not be U.S.

citizens, as evidenced by honorees like Mother Teresa in 1985, German chancellor Angela Merkel in 2011 and former UK prime ministers Margaret Thatcher in 1991 and Tony Blair in 2009.

AMERICAN HERO. John Glenn (*opposite*) had the good fortune of the mathematical skills of Katherine Johnson (*above and inset*), who, along with other African American women, computed the requirements of his orbital mission. She was honored on November 24, 2015, as was Willie Mays, seated beside her. *Opposite:* The president presents Glenn with his medal, May 24, 2012.

2009–2016 MEDAL OF FREEDOM RECIPIENTS.

During his time in office President Obama awarded 117 medals, the most ever, followed by Ronald Reagan's 102. Obama's final list demonstrates the incredible diversity of recipients over these years.

AUGUST 12, 2009
Nancy Goodman
   Brinker
Dr. Pedro José
   Greer Jr.
Stephen Hawking
Rep. Jack Kemp*
Sen. Edward Kennedy
Billie Jean King
Reverend Joseph
   Lowery
Joseph Medicine
   Crow
Harvey Milk*
Justice Sandra Day
   O'Connor
Sidney Poitier
Chita Rivera
Mary Robinson
Dr. Janet Davison
   Rowley
Archbishop Desmond
   Tutu
Muhammad Yunus

FEBRUARY 15, 2011
John H. Adams
Maya Angelou
Warren Buffett
President George
   H. W. Bush
Jasper Johns
Gerda Weissmann
   Klein
Rep. John Lewis
Dr. Tom Little*
Yo-Yo Ma
Sylvia Mendez
Angela Merkel
Stan Musial
Bill Russell
Jean Kennedy Smith
John J. Sweeney

JUNE 30, 2011
Robert M. Gates

MAY 29, 2012
Madeleine Albright
John Doar
Bob Dylan

Dr. William Foege
John Glenn
Gordon Hirabayashi*
Dolores Huerta
Jan Karski
Juliette Gordon Low*
Toni Morrison
Justice John Paul
   Stevens
Pat Summitt

JUNE 13, 2012
Shimon Peres

NOVEMBER 20, 2013
Ernie Banks
Ben Bradlee
Bill Clinton
Sen. Daniel Inouye*
Daniel Kahneman
Sen. Richard Lugar
Loretta Lynn
Mario Molina
Sally Ride*
Bayard Rustin*
Arturo Sandoval
Dean Smith
Gloria Steinem
Cordy Tindell "C.T."
   Vivian
Patricia Wald
Oprah Winfrey

NOVEMBER 24, 2014
Alvin Ailey
Isabel Allende
Tom Brokaw
James Chaney*
Mildred Dresselhaus
Rep. John Dingell
Andrew Goodman*
Ethel Kennedy
Suzan Harjo
Rep. Abner Mikva
Rep. Patsy Takemoto
   Mink*
Rep. Edward Roybal*
Michael Schwerner*
Charles Sifford
Robert Solow
Meryl Streep

Marlo Thomas
Stevie Wonder

NOVEMBER 24, 2015
Yogi Berra*
Bonnie Carroll
Rep. Shirley
   Chisholm*
Emilio Estefan
Gloria Estefan
Billy Frank Jr.*
Rep. Lee Hamilton
Katherine G. Johnson
Willie Mays
Sen. Barbara Mikulski
Itzhak Perlman
William Ruckelshaus
Stephen Sondheim
Steven Spielberg
Barbra Streisand
James Taylor
Minoru Yasui*

NOVEMBER 22, 2016
Kareem Abdul-Jabbar
Elouise Cobell*
Ellen DeGeneres
Robert De Niro
Richard Garwin
Bill and Melinda
   Gates
Frank Gehry
Margaret H.
   Hamilton
Tom Hanks
Grace Hopper*
Michael Jordan
Maya Lin
Lorne Michaels
Newt Minow
Eduardo Padrón
Robert Redford
Diana Ross
Vin Scully
Bruce Springsteen
Cicely Tyson

JANUARY 12, 2017
Vice President
   Joseph R. Biden Jr.**

*Awarded posthumously
**Awarded with Distinction

Opposite, left column (t–b):
Meryl Streep, Kareem Abdul-Jabaar, Tom Hanks, Pat Summitt, Bill Clinton.

Opposite, right column:
Bill and Melinda Gates, Ellen DeGeneres, Maya Angelou, Bob Dylan.

This page:
THE PRESIDENT AWARDED the Medal of Freedom to a surprised Vice President Joe Biden at an event that had been described simply as a toast to senior staff. It was bestowed "with Distinction," a level of veneration previously reserved for just three others—Pope John Paul II, President Ronald Reagan, and General Colin Powell.

by BOB TEWKSBURY

Bob Tewksbury *gives us the professional ballplayer's view on the president's pitching prowess—or lack thereof.*

#5. Barack Obama
April 5, 2010
"He looked like he could have used some mental skills coaching before he took the mound—my, did he look scared. Okay . . . not all bashing. I love his loyalty to the South Side of Chicago, donning the White Sox cap when he got to the mound. But then things get interesting again. If he were pitching a game, the president would have committed no fewer than four or five balks before throwing a pitch! When he finally starts his delivery to throw the pitch, his lower half actually looks pretty good . . . until . . . he breaks his hands and his arm. Ugh, his arm! It looks like it'd been injected with Novocain. It simply doesn't function. It's almost as if it's not even part of his body. In fairness, I think he did a remarkable job just getting it close to the plate. But in the big leagues it ain't about "close," Mr. President. I can and did throw a pitch just like you did—but for a strike: it was called the 'Eephus pitch.'"

#4. John F. Kennedy
April 10, 1961
"Okay so he threw it from the stands, but still enough to show a good arm action. Despite his famous back troubles, you can tell this man was an athlete."

#3. Jimmy Carter
October 28, 1995
"Wow. He threw the ball harder than I did! Then he gets a hug from Jane Fonda . . . really! All things considered, a pretty good outing."

#2. George H. W. Bush
April 3, 1989
"Reminded me of Jim Kaat. Bush senior, a former captain and first baseman of Yale University's baseball team, played in two College World Series, so he's no stranger to the game—work fast and throw strikes. Love it!"

#1. George W. Bush
October 30, 2001
"No pressure: this was only game three of a World Series at Yankee Stadium and just six weeks after 9/11. But talk about body language! 'W' walked to the mound like he was Nolan Ryan and, despite wearing a bulletproof vest and the distraction of the accompanying Secret

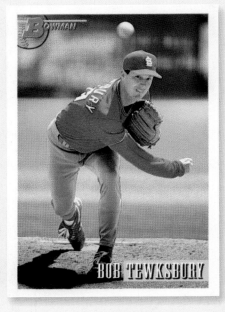

Service agent *dressed as an umpire*, proceeded to throw an effortless strike with total conviction! Very impressive! Without question the best of all time."

At the 2010 White House Correspondent's Dinner, President Obama gave us yet another pair of tongue-in-cheek opinions. "A few weeks ago I was able to throw out the first pitch at the Washington Nationals game. I don't know if you saw it, but I threw it a little high and a little outside. This is how FOX News covered it: 'President panders to extreme left-wing of batter's box.' On the other hand,

MSNBC had a different take—'President pitches no-hitter.'"

———

Bob Tewksbury was drafted by the New York Yankees in 1981 and spent 13 seasons in the major leagues with six teams: the Yankees, Cubs, Cardinals, Rangers, Padres, and Twins. A 1992 All-Star with 110 career victories, Bob was notorious for his Eephus pitch. In one 1998 game, Tewksbury, pitching for the Twins, resorted to lobbing balls at Cardinals' slugger Mark McGwire, and it worked: the major league home-run leader could only laugh as he grounded out and popped up on the 44-mph pitches.

NO MOMENT GOES UNCRITICIZED, even the ceremonial first pitch. This time it was the "mom jeans" and looping pitch, at a Major League Baseball All-Star game in St. Louis, July 2009.

THE DIGITAL PRESIDENCY

With a two-term limit (2,920 days), timing can be everything in shaping a president's legacy. Some step onto the economic carousel when it is booming, but others are not so lucky: for example, three of the last six U.S. presidents—Ronald Reagan, George W. Bush, and Barack Obama—inherited recessions as they stepped into the Oval Office. Barack Obama, however, also inherited a second industrial revolution that was every bit as dramatic as the first, except this one was driven by digital technology rather than water and steam. The first revolution took the better part of a century to play out; this one has taken less than a decade. The first "'smartphone,'" arrived on the market in 2007. By the end of 2017, it is estimated that there will be 220 million smartphone users in the U.S. alone—that's 63.5 percent of the population.

So whatever else history might ascribe to the Obama years, there's no questioning the fact that he will be remembered as the first "'social media president.'" He posted his first "presidential tweet" (for an American Red Cross Haiti appeal) in 2010, and, for a non-digital native, he's come a long way since then. Obama and his social media team have embraced every opportunity to make digital outreach work for them—particularly when it comes to reaching young voters. Look at the sea of joyful selfies that he generates everywhere he goes (see opposite and pages 152, 154, and 155).

In 2015, Obama became the first president to have a Twitter handle (@POTUS), the first to go live from the Oval Office on Facebook, and the first to answer questions from citizens on YouTube. In addition to being the first African American president, Barack Obama has also been dubbed as the first ever "political-pop culture celebrity." Who would ever have guessed that the president could generate more Twitter followers than, well, just about everyone? At time of writing, his 83 million @BarackObama followers are only surpassed by Taylor Swift with 83.2, Justin Bieber with 91.4, and Katy Perry with 95.4. The other public figure making quite a name for himself with his tweets was well down in the rankings, at 21.5 million. ★

Previous pages:
THE U.S. WOMEN'S National Soccer Team poses for a group selfie with the president in the East Room to celebrate their victory in the 2015 FIFA Women's World Cup, October 27, 2015.

Opposite:
PRESIDENT OBAMA TAKES a selfie with 11-year-old Jacob Haynes and four-year-old James Haynes after taking a family photograph with departing White House staffer Heather Foster, December 4, 2015.

Opposite:

THE PRESIDENT POSES for a selfie with Bill Nye "The Science Guy" and astrophysicist Neil Degrasse Tyson in the Blue Room before the White House Student Film Festival, February 28, 2014.

Above:

PRESIDENT OBAMA TWEETING at his laptop during a Twitter Town Hall in the East Room of the White House, July 6, 2011.

Clockwise from opposite, top left:

OBAMA MEETING WITH service members during
a visit to MacDill Air Force Base, Tampa, Florida,
September 17, 2014; posing with diners at Magnolia's
Deli & Café during the College Affordability Bus Tour,
Rochester, New York, August 22, 2013; striking the
Heisman Trophy pose with Heisman Trophy winner
Derrick Henry at the conclusion of the National Prayer
Breakfast, Washington, D.C., February 4, 2016; using
a GoPro® on a selfie stick during a hike to view the Exit
Glacier during a visit to the Kenai Fjords National Park,
Seward, Alaska, September 1, 2015.

PATRICK MCQUOWN

Patrick McQuown *is trained in Forensic Sciences and is a tech-entrepreneur. He is the Executive Director of the Center for Entrepreneurship at James Madison University and a former professor at Brown University.*

Just before 3 A.M. EST, Singlepoint, the mobile messaging startup for which I worked at the time, had to make a decision: Broadcast a text message to millions of people at this ungodly hour, or wait? It was August 23, 2008, and text messaging had only recently become a primary channel of consumer messaging. Twitter, which played a significant role in the 2016 election, was in its infancy, and SnapChat was yet to be conceived.

What made sending a message in the early morning hours so critical was the fact that wireless carriers had strict policies about text messaging: no text messages could be sent from a brand or content owner to any consumer after 10 P.M. EST. Breaking this rule could end our access to the carriers. We were five hours past that deadline, and if we sent the text, we were putting our entire business at risk. However, this specific text was different. It was historic. After minimal internal debate, we hit send. Simultaneously, millions of mobile phones

across the country lit up with the message: "Barack has chosen Senator Joe Biden to be our VP nominee. Watch the first Obama-Biden rally live at 3 pm ET on www. BarackObama.com. Spread the word!"

With that click of a button, Barack Obama announced to his millions of supporters his pick of Joe Biden via text message—before the traditional press knew about it—in 2008; a truly breakthrough move. The subsequent campaign's use of modern communications technology to interact directly with citizens had powerful implications for democracy. Eight years after that message was sent and shortly after a tumultuous 2016 presidential election, we are still struggling to understand the impact technology such as the Web, mobile messaging, and social media is having on our democracy, both positive and negative.

I was proud to be part of that historic mobile campaign for our 44th president, and based on my time working with many of his core campaign team, I knew we were in for something good. In 2013, when the Net Neutrality debate started, the president selected a friend of mine, Tom Wheeler, to take the helm of the Federal Communications

Commission. The debate focused on whether the Internet is a public good, like telephone and broadcast systems, and if it should be similarly regulated. A poor decision on this issue would stymie the innovation that the Internet had created. Throughout the months of debate, I never lost faith that the outcome would benefit our nation. I had come to know Tom, working closely with him to help the wireless carriers expand messaging with the introduction of mobile campaigns, like *American Idol* text polling. These early mobile initiatives created the massive messaging ecosystem we now know. Sure enough, Tom led the FCC to its historic decision on Net Neutrality, allowing the Internet to remain a powerful driver of innovation and technological change.

From the start of his first presidential campaign, Barack Obama and his administration have been at the forefront of the rapid technological wave that has heavily influenced political discourse in this country. The Internet, mobile technology, and the tools spawned from them—the Web, social media, push messaging, etc.—are now ingrained in our political process, even though we are still trying to figure out how to use it to strengthen our democracy rather than divide us. I believe that if we continue to follow the example of Obama and his administration, we have a good chance of getting it right.

———

PROFESSOR PATRICK MCQUOWN teaching at Brown University, Providence, Rhode Island.

LinkedIn

Above: THE OBAMAS GREET guests at the Congressional Black Caucus Foundation's 46th Annual Legislative Conference Phoenix Awards Dinner, Washington, D.C., September 17, 2016.

Below: PRESIDENT OBAMA SPEAKS to audience members with LinkedIn CEO Jeff Weiner during a town hall meeting at the Computer History Museum in Mountain View, California, September 26, 2011.

TWEETS
327

FOLLOWING
72

Tweets   Tweets & repli

President Obama ✔
@POTUS

Dad, husband, and 44th President of the United States. Tweets may be archived: wh.gov/privacy.

📍 Washington, D.C.
🔗 WhiteHouse.gov
📅 Joined June 2013
🎈 Born on August 4, 1961

 Tweet to President Oba...

📷 61 Photos and videos

President Obama @P
Proud of our
who prove tha
no more pow

↩ 1.3K ⟲ 7K

 President Obama @
Today, we ho
the fight agai

 President Obama ✔
@POTUS

⚙ 👤 Follow

Hello, Twitter! It's Barack. Really! Six years in, they're finally giving me my own account.

RETWEETS   LIKES
279,533   421,130

LIKES
3

⚙ Following

Who to follow · Refresh · View all

Hillary Clinton ✓ @Hil... ✕
👤 Follow

Barack Obama ✓ @... ✕
👤 Follow

The First Lady ✓ @F... ✕
👤 Follow

Find friends

Trends · Change

#TRANSFORMERS
Two worlds collide in one epic trailer.
📷 Promoted by #TRANSFORMERS

Chris Sale
Red Sox deal top prospects to land pitching ace Chris Sale

#TrumpCabinetBand
4,561 Tweets

#GrammyNominations
353K Tweets

Air Force One
Trump says 'cancel order!' for Boeing's Air Force One

#HighSchoolForMeWas

ns of Change - folks
America, there's
than that of citizen.

who are leading
DS. Because of

Opposite, bottom:
THE PRESIDENT'S FIRST tweet from May 18, 2015, with the handle "@POTUS." President Obama was the first president to have a Twitter account.

Middle:
THE TWITTER PAGE for Barack Obama as seen in December 2016.

Above:
PRESIDENT OBAMA LEADING the public, family, and civil rights leaders to the Edmund Pettis Bridge in Selma, Alabama, March 7, 2015, to mark the 50th anniversary of the marches from Selma to Montgomery.

THE WHITE HOUSE CORRESPONDENTS' DINNER

HOSTED BY THE White House Correspondents' Association, the organization that represents the White House press corps, the annual White House Correspondents' Dinner (WHCD) is a black-tie event where journalists mingle with Hollywood celebrities, superstar athletes, and politicos and is perennially one of Washington's hottest tickets.

The first ever Correspondents' Dinner in 1921 was an all-male event held with just 50 in attendance. It was another three years before a president—at the time, Calvin Coolidge—set a precedent that has seen every sitting president attend the dinner at least once during his term in office.

Guests of color were barred from the WHCD until the 1950s. Women first attended in 1962 but only after the legendary Helen Thomas—the first female White House reporter—had threatened a boycott until the rules changed; bowing to the pressure, JFK soon obliged.

The 1980s saw the beginning of the dinner's transformation from an exclusive night of Washington insiders and musical performance—with legendary performers like Frank Sinatra and Nat King Cole—to a celebrity-filled extravaganza with the focus on edgy political satire.

Piano-playing satirist Mark Russell set the comedy trend when he headlined in 1983, and there has been no looking back since. The format is certainly different. For once, the President of the United States plays the role of a warm-up act. He will inevitably get his humorous shots in at the media and others but then introduces the headliner—a celebrity comedian. In what is surely the ultimate affirmation that First Amendments rights are still alive and well, a no-holds-barred POTUS roast is always on the menu. ★

THE PRESIDENT IS JOINED at the podium by "Luther," his outspoken "anger translator," played by *Key & Peele*'s Keegan-Michael Key, April 25, 2015.

Jokes from THE PRESIDENT

"Tonight reminds us that we are lucky to live in a country where reporters get to give a head of state a hard time on a daily basis and then, once a year, give him or her the chance, at least, to try to return the favor." —2014

"All this change hasn't been easy. Change never is. So I've cut the tension by bringing a new friend to the White House. He's warm, he's cuddly, loyal, enthusiastic. You just have to keep him on a tight leash. Every once in a while he goes charging off in the wrong direction and gets himself into trouble. But enough about Joe Biden." —2009

"Even though the mainstream press gives me a hard time, I hear I'm still pretty big on Twitter and Facebook—or as Sarah Palin calls it, the 'socialized media.'" —2010

"I am very much looking forward to hearing Seth Meyers tonight. He's a young, fresh face who can do no wrong in the eyes of his fans. Seth, enjoy it while it lasts." —2011

"Recently [Governor Mitt Romney's] campaign criticized me for slow-jamming the news with Jimmy Fallon. In fact, I understand Governor Romney was so incensed, he asked his staff if he could get some equal time on *The Merv Griffin Show*." —2012

"The fact is I really do respect the press. I recognize that the press and I have different jobs to do. My job is to be president; your job is to keep me humble. Frankly, I think I'm doing my job better." —2013

"While talking sports, just last month, a wonderful story—an American won the Boston Marathon for first time in 30 years. Which was inspiring and only fair, since a Kenyan has been president for the last six. Had to even things out." —2014

"Six years into my presidency some people still say that I'm arrogant, aloof, condescending. Some people are so dumb." —2015

"In my final year, my approval ratings keep going up. The last time I was this high, I was trying to decide on my major." —2016

THE HOSTS. *Top row, left to right:* Conan O'Brian, Cecily Strong, Jimmy Kimmel; *Middle row, left to right:* Wanda Sykes, Seth Meyers, Bernie Sanders in the audience; *Bottom row, left to right:* Joel McHale, Larry Wilmore, Jay Leno.

Jokes from THE HOSTS OF THE WHITE HOUSE CORRESPONDENTS' DINNER

"If you told me when I was a kid I'd be standing on a dais with President Barack Obama, I would have said, 'The president's name is Barack Obama?'"—*Jimmy Kimmel*, 2012

"C'mon? First black president playing basketball— I mean that's one step forward, two steps back! . . . Nobody's going to give the president a hard foul with the Secret Service standing there." —*Wanda Sykes*, 2009

"And according to the Pentagon, al-Qaeda is in financial ruin. You know what broke them? Health insurance premiums!"—*Jay Leno*, 2010

"This event has grown past Washington, and many Hollywood celebrities are also here tonight. Jon Hamm is here. He looks the way every Republican thinks they look. And Zach Galifianakis is also here: he looks the way Republicans think every Democrat looks." —*Seth Meyers*, 2011

"You can't have a beer with Romney, because he doesn't drink. You can't have a cup of coffee with him, because he can't have caffeine. You can't even play Monopoly with him, because he keeps trying to put the dog on the car." —*Jimmy Kimmel*, 2012

"It's an honor to share this stage with the president. When you think about it, the president and I are a lot alike. We both went to Harvard, we both have two children, and we both told Joe Biden we didn't have extra tickets for tonight's event."—*Conan O'Brien*, 2013

"Thanks to Obamacare—or as the president refers to it, 'me-care' —millions of newly insured young Americans can visit the doctor's office and see what a print magazine actually looks like." —*Joel McHale*, 2014

"Seriously, you gotta give Mitch McConnell credit. At this point he could block LeBron James. He's unbelievable."— *Larry Gilmore*, 2016

PRESIDENT OBAMA REACTS to a joke at the White House Correspondents' Dinner, April 27, 2013.

PRESIDENT OBAMA APPEARS on *The Colbert Report* at a taping in the Lisner Auditorium at George Washington University in Washington, D.C., December 8, 2014. The backdrop is a portrait of host Stephen Colbert as President Lincoln.

Opposite, clockwise from top left: **ENJOYING A BACKSTAGE** joke with Jay Leno, October 2011; *Late Night* laughter with David Letterman, September 2012; bending Jimmy Fallon's ear on *Late Night*, April 2012; cracking up on *Jimmy Kimmel Live*, October 2016.

PRESIDENT LINCOLN

LATE-NIGHT TELEVISION

For most of the first half of the twentieth century, radio ruled the airwaves. Then, on April 30, 1939, from the opening ceremonies of the World's Fair in New York, Franklin Delano Roosevelt became the first U.S. president to make an appearance on (black-and-white) television. Surprisingly it would be another eight years before, Harry S. Truman became the first U.S. president to give a live address from the White House, in October 1947. His subject? Asking Americans to cut back on their use of grain to help starving Europeans. Since that time, every U.S. president has made progressively good use of television for straight political purposes, and yet strangely—considering that *The Tonight Show* with Steve Allen debuted in 1954—it was not until March 2009 that, by appearing on NBC's *The Tonight Show* with Jay Leno, Barack Obama became the first ever sitting U.S. president to appear on late-night television. That's a full 70 years after FDR's first use of the (then) new medium. Presidential candidates aplenty had made appearances on comedy shows—like Nixon's disastrous appearance on *Rowan & Martin's Laugh-In* and Bill Clinton wearing shades and playing his saxophone on *The Arsenio Hall Show*—but never a sitting president. Over the next eight years, President Obama would become a much sought-after late-night guest with—as can be seen in the pictures on these two pages—many memorable moments of great television. ★

KNOCK KNOCK

THE HIT CRACKLE TV series *Comedians in Cars Getting Coffee*, created and hosted by comedian Jerry Seinfeld, premiered in 2012. In each episode Seinfeld introduces a vintage car to a fellow comedian and the comedic banter flows as they drive somewhere for coffee. But then, in Episode 1 of Season 7, which aired December 30, 2015, Jerry's choice of guest was a surprising break with tradition.

According to Tammy Johnston, an executive producer at Embassy Row Productions, "The idea of inviting Obama to be on the show came out of an 'ideal guest' conversation, and the president was top of Jerry's wish list. So I made a call." When a "yes" came in, the shoot had to be scheduled not only around the president's busy schedule but also unpredictable world events. Once on site, the *Comedians in Cars* crew had to work around the strict White House security and—rather than the

normal four-hour shoot—they had a tight 90 minutes scheduled with the president.

En route to the White House driving an iconic 1963 split-window 'Vette, Jerry explains to viewers how "The commander in chief has gotten off just enough funny lines to qualify for getting on this show." What follows is quite remarkable.

For both the president and Jerry—and over ten million viewers on multiple platforms—it was a very special experience. As the president glowingly noted on screen, "You know what, [driving this car] is a childhood dream." Jerry meanwhile would later say, "Knocking on the Oval Office window was probably the peak of my existence." ★

Above: JERRY SEINFIELD KNOCKS on the window of the Oval Office to kick off the episode.

This picture:
MAKING JERRY LAUGH . . .
Having drunk from a paper cup
delivered to him by a secret service
agent, the president deadpans,
"That's just a little gin I take midday."

Below:
. . . AND KEEP LAUGHING.
During their ride around the
White House grounds, the
president confides, " I do really well
with the zero-to-eight-year-old
demographic—they love me. Partly
because I think my ears are big."

ROCKIN' THE WHITE HOUSE

OR ALL THE RIGORS, trials, and tribulations that come with the job of POTUS, one very pleasant consolation is the ability to invite your favorite performers to "drop by" the White House from time to time. While, perhaps as a result of his own Hollywood roots, Ronald Reagan was the president to avail himself of this opportunity more than any other in recent times, the Obamas, too, had a steady stream of musical notaries performing in their D.C. "crib."

Most of them came to perform for the PBS series, *In Performance at the White House* but others came for state dinners and some for private, personally funded soirees. The list of performers has ranged from current-day superstars like Beyoncé, Kendrick Lamar, Rhianna, and Jay Z to venerated music industry veterans such as Aretha Franklin, Jose Feliciano, and Stevie Wonder.

You may be surprised to see which performers have been the Obamas' most frequent musical guests during their eight years in the White House. . . . ★

Above: **THE PRESIDENT DESCRIBING** his teenage memories of Led Zeppelin to the surviving members of the band—John Paul Jones, Robert Plant, and Jimmy Page, at the Kennedy Center Honors, December 12, 2012.

Opposite: **SATISFACTION FOR ROLLING STONE,** Sir Mick Jagger must be performing at the White House— Red, White and Blues concert, February 21, 2012.

Most Frequent PERFORMERS AT THE WHITE HOUSE

COMMON: The rapper turned actor, activist, and Academy Award–winner, who, like Michelle Obama, calls the South Side of Chicago home, has certainly been at home in the White House with five visits, including:
- A Celebration of American Poetry, May 11, 2011
- A Salute to the Troops, November 6, 2014
- *Selma* movie screening, January 15, 2015

JAMES TAYLOR: The ever-popular singer-songwriter, famous for hits such as "You've Got a Friend" and "Fire and Rain," is another clear favorite, having visited the White House on five occasions:
- Germany State Dinner, June 7, 2011
- *In Performance: Country Music*, November 16, 2011
- National Tree Lighting, December 6, 2012
- Prince and Stevie Wonder concert, June 19, 2015
- *In Performance: American Creativity*, January 8, 2016

JOHN LEGEND: The activist and Grammy-winning singer, who won an Oscar with Common for their song "Glory" from the movie *Selma*, has made three White House appearances:
- *In Performance: A Celebration of Music from the Civil Rights Movement*, February 9, 2010
- United Kingdom State Dinner, March 14, 2012
- President Obama's 55th birthday party, August 8, 2016

STEVIE WONDER: The inimitable Motown and R&B legend has major fans in POTUS and FLOTUS, particularly for their more intimate, "we-paid-with-our-own-funds" events:
- Motown Sound, February 24, 2011
- Prince and Stevie Wonder concert, June 19, 2015
- President Obama's 55th birthday party, August 8, 2016

QUEEN LATIFAH: In the late '80s/early '90s she was a chart-topping rapper and the star of the sitcom *Living Single* before going on to her own daytime talk show and an Oscar nomination for her role in *Chicago*. She has made three White House appearances:
- *In Performance: A Celebration of Music from the Civil Rights Movement*, February 9, 2010
- *In Performance: Memphis Soul*, April 9, 2013
- *In Performance: American Creativity*, January 8, 2016

Top row (l–r): Kris Kristofferson and James Taylor; Aretha Franklin; Stevie Wonder.

Second row (l–r): Willie Nelson; Sir Paul McCartney; Beyoncé.

Bottom row (l–r): Bruce Springsteen—the other Boss—hams it up with President Obama; Dianne Reeves; B. B. King.

THE FIRST FAMILY

Raising two teenage girls is a challenge wherever one lives—but raising them in the White House? That surely brings a whole different set of issues, especially when your living quarters sit atop the most powerful and busiest government offices on the planet. Well, it seems that isn't the case for the Obamas. Washington insiders frequently remark on how the First Family calmly managed to keep family first. When in D.C., the president's 6:30 P.M. family dinner was sacrosanct, as evidenced by tongue-in-cheek comments like, "It had better be a national emergency or something to take me away from my dinner with the family." Michelle added, "It wasn't until the White House and we were together seven days a week that he had time to coach the girls' teams and go to all their events."

As the first African American family to live at 1600 Pennsylvania Avenue, the world was perhaps paying even more attention than normal as to how the 43rd residents—Washington did not live there—would conduct themselves in "The People's House." And the consensus has been unanimously positive: the Obamas have been lauded for their open-door policy, inclusiveness, love of a really good party, and discreet sense of unassuming style.

It has been said that "behind every great man is a great woman." In the Obamas' case, that might more accurately read, "*beside* every great man." . . . When campaigning, Michelle Obama's skills at persuading undecided voters earned her the nickname "The Closer.'" When not playing the role of mother, wife, or hostess at state dinners and other events, the First Lady quickly set about using her influence and closing skills by pushing through an incredible list of her own initiatives. Focusing on children's causes, in 2010 she launched the Let's Move! program to tackle childhood obesity. The school lunch program, which provides free and reduced–price meals for over 20 million low-income-family children followed, as did a multitude of other initiatives, like working with the USTA to refurbish over 6,000 kid's tennis courts and train 12,000 coaches for junior tennis.

Returning to the "real world," the Obamas—and their two dogs—are remaining in D.C., at least until daughter Sasha graduates from Sidwell Friends School while Malia takes a gap year before heading to Harvard. From the outside, their new 8,200-square-foot rental home in the Kalorama neighborhood of Washington couldn't be more different to their previous address, but on the inside, the family's life will continue without missing a beat. ★

Previous pages:
THE OBAMAS in front of the spectacular 2,400-foot Yosemite Falls, Yosemite National Park, July 19, 2016.

Opposite:
THE PRESIDENT, First Lady, and daughter Sasha order ice cream at Bruster's in Panama City Beach, Florida, August 15, 2010.

Above: FIRST LADY MICHELLE OBAMA hugs daughters Sasha and Malia during their visit to the Great Wall of China, March 23, 2014.

Left: PRESIDENT OBAMA and his daughters at the White House, October 2009.

Opposite, left column (t–b):
THE OBAMAS WALK along the White House Colonnade, September 21, 2010; 106-year-old Virginia McLaurin achieves her dream of meeting the Obamas, February 22, 2016; the Obamas prepare to meet trick-or-treaters at the North Portico of the White House on Halloween in Washington, D.C., on October 31, 2009

Opposite, right column (t–b):
THE OBAMAS PARTICIPATE in a tree planting at the Kenilworth Aquatic Gardens, Washington, D.C., April 21, 2009; Michelle Obama, President Hu Jintao of China, and President Obama at a State Dinner at the White House, Washington, January 19, 2011; the president gives Michelle a kiss for the "Kiss Cam" at an Olympic men's exhibition basketball game while Malia Obama and Joe Biden watch on the jumbotron, Washington, D.C., July 16, 2012.

Opposite, top: THE FIRST LADY gives her final speech to honor the 2017 School Counselor of the Year in the East Room of the White House, January 6, 2017.

Opposite, below: MICHELLE OBAMA is assisted by students during the spring planting in the White House kitchen garden, April 9, 2009.

Above: DURING FILMING OF an episode of Carpool Karaoke, Michelle rocks out with James Corden of the *Late Late Show*, July 21, 2016. Missy Elliott later joined the ride to sing "This Is For My Girls," a song promoting Mrs. Obama's Let Girls Learn global education initiative.

Right: IN SUPPORT OF her Let's Move! initiative, the First Lady joins in a performance of the #GimmeFive dance during the annual Easter Egg Roll at the White House, April 6, 2015.

THE OBAMAS dance to
Earth, Wind & Fire at the
Governors' Ball, the White
House, February 22, 2009.

Opposite:
THE PRESIDENT hugs the First
Lady after she introduced him at a
campaign event in Davenport, Iowa,
August 15, 2012.

"Michelle LaVaughn Robinson, girl of the South Side—for the past 25 years, you have not only been my wife and mother of my children, you have been my best friend. You took on a role you didn't ask for and you made it your own, with grace and with grit and with style and good humor. You made the White House a place that belongs to everybody. And the new generation sets its sights higher because it has you as a role model. So you have made me proud. And you have made the country proud."

—BARACK OBAMA from his Farewell Address, January 10, 2017

BEING OBAMA

ANYONE WHO THINKS the job of president of the United States isn't a tough one need look no further than the above picture and then compare it to the one on the right. Note the graying of the president's hair: eight years as Leader of the Free World takes its follicular toll. This happens with just about every president, but, with the possible exception of JFK, very few of them have refused to let "the burden of office" visibly weigh down their spirits in the way Barack Obama did. Make no mistake, it's a 24/365 job.

There is nothing in the job description, however, that says incumbents shouldn't do their very best to spread a little joy, optimism, and yes, even laughter when spontaneous opportunities present themselves. The random "Kodak moments" captured on the coming pages and throughout this book show a president—and family—that, rather than being full of itself, reveled in every opportunity to seize those moments. Whether it was allowing Spider-Man (in the form of a White House staffer's young son) to enmesh him, having Stephen Colbert tutor him on interview skills when applying for his next job, or joking about his big ears, Barack Obama was a natural master of the art of being simultaneously engaging, warm, funny, and outgoing while always managing to remain presidential. ★

Above: VISITING THE OVAL office on May 8, 2009, a White House staffer's young son told the president he'd just had his hair cut, then innocently asked if he could feel the president's head to see if it felt the same as his.

Opposite: PRESIDENT OBAMA JOKINGLY mimics McKayla Maroney's trademark smirk, November 17, 2012. Maroney is part of the "fierce five" U.S. women's Olympic gymnastics team.

ENERGY A PLAYFUL moment in the Oval Office, a staffer's "Spider-Man" son enmeshes a very willing victim, January 26, 2012.

Following page, clockwise from top left:
THE PRESIDENT kneels on the floor to say hi to the baby daughter of Deputy National Security Advisor Ben Rhodes, June 4, 2013; Obama greets children from the Valleyland Kids summer program in Chatfield, Minnesota, during a three-day bus tour in the Midwest, 2011; "Wow, is it really you?" Four-year-old Malik Hall can't believe who he has just met on a White House visit, September 4, 2015; Obama hugs Mari Copeny backstage at Northwestern High School in Flint, Michigan, May 4, 2016; "Who're you pointing at?" The president goofs around with Marine Corps families in Hawaii, Christmas Day, 2014; posing with Girl Scout Troup 2612 from Tulsa during the annual White House Science Fair, May 24, 2014.

VOICES

STEPHANIE *and* BRIAN TOBE

Stephanie *and* Brian Tobe *(above) recount the surprise visitor at their wedding at the Lodge at Torrey Pines in La Jolla, California.*

I was completely overcome with emotion—not only was I getting married that day, but I was about to meet someone my soon-to-be husband and I had admired for years: President Barack Obama.

Never in our wildest dreams did we imagine our small wedding would include such an honored guest. We were waiting patiently for our wedding ceremony to start, watching as President Obama finished his golf game and hoping he might see us from our suite's window.

Realizing it might be our only chance, we ran through the corridors of the Lodge at Torrey Pines to our ceremony site next to the 18th hole, hoping to get a glimpse of our president as he graciously shook hands with our wedding guests. Once outside, all of our guests instead turned in our direction, parted ways, and cheered us on as we ran across the lawn. I never thought I'd be able to run so easily in heels and a heavy wedding dress, but this once-in-a-lifetime chance made me feel like I was floating on air. President Obama was so friendly, taking our hands and giving us congratulatory hugs. I had no words, only tears of joy and a "thank you." What was always going to be a meaningful day for my husband and I became that much more memorable.

—

A BEAMING Stephanie and Brian Tobe rush to greet President Obama, who stopped in at their wedding, October 2015.

This page:
NBA LEGEND Shaquille O'Neal appears to tower over the president during a visit to the Oval Office, February 27, 2015.

Opposite, top:
PRESIDENT OBAMA and the First Lady play some very convincing monsters as they read the classic children's book *Where the Wild Things Are* by Maurice Sendak, March 28, 2016.

Opposite, bottom:
CAROLINE KENNEDY SCHLOSSBERG stands beside the same desk her father JFK used in the Oval Office while the president jokingly looks for her late brother, John F. Kennedy Jr., who, in an iconic photo, was pictured under the desk as a child, March 9, 2009.

FAREWELL
ADDRESS

January 10, 2017 | CHICAGO, ILLINOIS

ELLO CHICAGO. It's good to be home. Thank you. . . . My fellow Americans—Michelle and I have been so touched by all the well wishes that we've received over the past few weeks. But tonight, it's my turn to say thanks. Whether we have seen eye to eye or rarely agreed at all, my conversations with you, the American people, in living rooms and in schools, at farms, on factory floors, at diners, and on distant military outposts—those conversations are what have kept me honest and kept me inspired and kept me going. And every day, I have learned from you. You made me a better president, and you made me a better man.

So I first came to Chicago when I was in my early twenties. And I was still trying to figure out who I was, still searching for a purpose in my life. And it was a neighborhood not far from here where I began working with church groups in the shadows of closed steel mills. It was on these streets where I witnessed the power of faith and the quiet dignity of working people in the face of struggle and loss. . . .

This is where I learned that change only happens when ordinary people get involved, and they get engaged, and they come together to demand it.

After eight years as your president, I still believe that. And it's not just my belief. It's the beating heart of our American idea— our bold experiment in self-government. It's the conviction that

---

PRESIDENT OBAMA MAKES his Farewell Address to the nation at the McCormick Center in Chicago, January 10, 2017.

we are all created equal, endowed by our Creator with certain unalienable rights, among them life, liberty, and the pursuit of happiness. It's the insistence that these rights, while self-evident, have never been self-executing; that "We, the People," through the instrument of our democracy, can form a more perfect union.

What a radical idea. A great gift that our Founders gave to us: the freedom to chase our individual dreams through our sweat and toil and imagination and the imperative to strive together, as well, to achieve a common good, a greater good.

For 240 years, our nation's call to citizenship has given work and purpose to each new generation. It's what led patriots to choose republic over tyranny, pioneers to trek west, slaves to brave that makeshift railroad to freedom. It's what pulled immigrants and refugees across oceans and the Rio Grande. It's what pushed women to reach for the ballot. It's what powered workers to organize. It's why GIs gave their lives at Omaha Beach and Iwo Jima, Iraq and Afghanistan. And why men and women from Selma to Stonewall were prepared to give theirs as well.

So that's what we mean when we say America is exceptional—not that our nation has been flawless from the start, but that we have shown the capacity to change and make life better for those who follow. Yes, our progress has been uneven. The work of democracy has always been hard. It's always been contentious. Sometimes it's been bloody. For every two steps forward, it often feels we take one step back. But the long sweep of America has been defined by forward motion, a constant widening of our founding creed to embrace all and not just some.

If I had told you eight years ago that America would reverse a great recession, reboot our auto industry, and unleash the longest stretch of job creation in our history; if I had told you that we would open up a new chapter with the Cuban people, shut down Iran's nuclear weapons program without firing a shot, take out the mastermind of 9/11; if I had told you that we would win marriage equality, and secure the right to health insurance for another 20 million of our fellow citizens—if I had told you all that, you might have said our sights were set a little too high. But that's what we did. That's what you did.

You were the change. You answered people's hopes, and because of you, by almost every measure, America is a better, stronger place than it was when we started.

In ten days, the world will witness a hallmark of our democracy—the peaceful transfer of power from one freely elected president to the next. I committed to President-elect Trump that my administration would ensure the smoothest possible transition, just as President Bush did for me. Because it's up to all of us to make sure our government can help us meet the many challenges we still face.

We have what we need to do so. We have everything we need to meet those challenges. After all, we remain the wealthiest, most powerful, and most respected nation on Earth. Our youth, our drive, our diversity and openness, our boundless capacity for risk and reinvention means that the future should be ours. But that potential will only be realized if our democracy works. Only if our politics better reflects the decency of our people. Only if all of us,

"You were the change. You answered people's hopes, and because of you, by almost every measure, America is a better, stronger place than it was when we started."

regardless of party affiliation or particular interests, help restore the sense of common purpose that we so badly need right now.

That's what I want to focus on tonight: the state of our democracy. Understand, democracy does not require uniformity. Our Founders argued. They quarreled. Eventually they compromised. They expected us to do the same. But they knew that democracy does require a basic sense of solidarity—the idea that for all our outward differences, we're all in this together; that we rise or fall as one.

There have been moments throughout our history that threaten that solidarity. And the beginning of this century has been one of those times. A shrinking world, growing inequality, demographic change, and the specter of terrorism—these forces haven't just tested our security and our prosperity but are testing our democracy as well. And how we meet these challenges to our democracy will determine our ability to educate our kids and create good jobs and protect our homeland. In other words, it will determine our future.

To begin with, our democracy won't work without a sense that everyone has economic opportunity. And the good news is that today the economy is growing again. Wages, incomes, home values, and retirement accounts are all rising again. Poverty is falling again. The wealthy are paying a fairer share of taxes even as the stock market shatters records. The unemployment rate is near a ten-year low. The uninsured rate has never, ever been lower. Health-care costs are rising at the slowest rate in 50 years. And I've said, and I mean it—if anyone can put together a plan that is demonstrably

A GRADUATE HOLDS up President Obama's book, *Dreams from My Father*, at the 148th Commencement Convocation at Howard University, Washington, D.C., May 7, 2016.

better than the improvements we've made to our health-care system and that covers as many people at less cost, I will publicly support it. Because that, after all, is why we serve. Not to score points or take credit but to make people's lives better.

But for all the real progress that we've made, we know it's not enough. Our economy doesn't work as well or grow as fast when a few prosper at the expense of a growing middle class and ladders for folks who want to get into the middle class. That's the economic argument. But stark inequality is also corrosive to our democratic ideal. While the top 1 percent has amassed a bigger share of wealth and income, too many families, in inner cities and in rural counties, have been left behind—the laid-off factory worker, the waitress or health-care worker who's just barely getting by and struggling to pay the bills, convinced that the game is fixed against them, that their government only serves the interests of the powerful—that's a recipe for more cynicism and polarization in our politics.

But there are no quick fixes to this long-term trend. I agree: our trade should be fair and not just free. But the next wave of economic dislocations won't come from overseas. It will come from the relentless pace of automation that makes a lot of good, middle-class jobs obsolete.

And so we're going to have to forge a new social compact to guarantee all our kids the education they need; to give workers the power to unionize for better wages; to update the social safety net to reflect the way we live now; and make more reforms to the tax code so corporations and individuals who reap the most from this new economy don't avoid their obligations to the country that's made their very success possible.

We can argue about how to best achieve these goals, but we can't be complacent about the goals themselves. For if we don't create opportunity for all people, the disaffection and division that has stalled our progress will only sharpen in years to come.

There's a second threat to our democracy—and this one is as old as our nation itself. After my election, there was talk of a post-racial America. And such a vision, however well-intended, was never realistic. Race remains a potent and often divisive force in our society. Now, I've lived long enough to know that race relations are better than they were ten or twenty or thirty years ago, no matter what some folks say. You can see it not just in statistics, you see it in the attitudes of young Americans across the political spectrum.

But we're not where we need to be. And all of us have more work to do. If every economic issue is framed as a struggle between a hardworking white middle class and an undeserving minority, then workers of all shades are going to be left fighting for scraps while the wealthy withdraw further into their private enclaves. If we're unwilling to invest in the children of immigrants just because they don't look like us, we will diminish the prospects of our own children—because those brown kids will represent a larger and larger share of America's workforce. And we have shown that our economy doesn't have to be a zero-sum game. Last year, incomes rose for all races, all age groups, for men and for women.

"All of us have more work to do. If every economic issue is framed as a struggle between a hardworking white middle class and an undeserving minority, then workers of all shades are going to be left fighting for scraps."

So if we're going to be serious about race going forward, we need to uphold laws against discrimination—in hiring and in housing and in education and in the criminal justice system. That is what our Constitution and our highest ideals require.

But laws alone won't be enough. Hearts must change. It won't change overnight. Social attitudes oftentimes take generations to change. But if our democracy is to work the way it should in this increasingly diverse nation, then each one of us need to try to heed the advice of a great character in American fiction—Atticus Finch—who said, "You never really understand a person until you consider things from his point of view . . . until you climb into his skin and walk around in it."

For blacks and other minority groups, it means tying our own very real struggles for justice to the challenges that a lot of people in this country face—not only the refugee or the immigrant or the rural poor or the transgender American, but also the middle-aged white guy who, from the outside, may seem like he's got advantages but has seen his world upended by economic and cultural and technological change. We have to pay attention and listen.

For white Americans, it means acknowledging that the effects of slavery and Jim Crow didn't suddenly vanish in the sixties—that when minority groups voice discontent, they're not just engaging in reverse racism or practicing political correctness. When they wage peaceful protest, they're not demanding special treatment but the equal treatment that our Founders promised.

For native-born Americans, it means reminding ourselves that the stereotypes about immigrants today were said, almost word for word, about the Irish and Italians and Poles—who it was said were going to destroy the fundamental character of America. And as it turned out, America wasn't weakened by the presence of these newcomers; these newcomers embraced this nation's creed, and this nation was strengthened.

So regardless of the station that we occupy, we all have to try harder. We all have to start with the premise that each of our fellow citizens loves this country just as much as we do; that they value hard work and family just like we do; that their children are just as curious and hopeful and worthy of love as our own.

And that's not easy to do. For too many of us, it's become safer to retreat into our own bubbles, whether in our neighborhoods, or on college campuses, or places of worship, or especially our social media feeds, surrounded by people who look like us and share the same political outlook and never challenge our assumptions. The rise of naked partisanship, and increasing economic and regional stratification, the splintering of our media into a channel for every taste—all this makes this great sorting seem natural, even inevitable. And increasingly, we become so secure in our bubbles that we start accepting only information, whether it's true or not, that fits our opinions instead of basing our opinions on the evidence that is out there.

And this trend represents a third threat to our democracy. But politics is a battle of ideas. That's how our democracy was designed. In the course of a healthy debate, we prioritize different goals and the different means of reaching them. But without some common baseline of facts, without a willingness to admit new information and concede that your opponent might be making a fair point and that science and reason

PRESIDENT OBAMA'S

FAREWELL ADDRESS

JANUARY 10, 2017

President Obama will give his farewell address in Chicago. Tune in here to watch on January 10, 2017.

matter—then we're going to keep talking past each other, and we'll make common ground and compromise impossible.

And isn't that part of what so often makes politics dispiriting? How can elected officials rage about deficits when we propose to spend money on preschool for kids but not when we're cutting taxes for corporations? How do we excuse ethical lapses in our own party, but pounce when the other party does the same thing? It's not just dishonest, this selective sorting of the facts; it's self-defeating. Because, as my mom used to tell me, reality has a way of catching up with you.

Take the challenge of climate change. In just eight years, we've halved our dependence on foreign oil; we've doubled our renewable energy; we've led the world to an agreement that has the promise to save this planet. But without bolder action, our children won't have time to debate the existence of climate change. They'll be busy dealing with its effects: more environmental disasters, more economic disruptions, waves of climate refugees seeking sanctuary.

Now, we can and should argue about the best approach to solve the problem. But to simply deny the problem not only betrays future generations, it betrays the essential spirit of this country—the essential spirit of innovation and practical problem-solving that guided our Founders. It is that spirit, born of the Enlightenment, that made us an economic powerhouse—the spirit that took flight at Kitty Hawk and Cape Canaveral; the spirit that cures disease and put a computer in every pocket. It's that spirit—a faith

Above:

THE WHITE HOUSE
web page announcing
President Obama's
Farewell Address.

Opposite:

PRESIDENT OBAMA
pauses during an
emotional moment of
the Farewell Address.

FAREWELL ADDRESS

in reason and enterprise and the primacy of right over might—that allowed us to resist the lure of fascism and tyranny during the Great Depression; that allowed us to build a post–World War II order with other democracies, an order based not just on military power or national affiliations but built on principles—the rule of law, human rights, freedom of religion, and speech, and assembly, and an independent press.

That order is now being challenged—first by violent fanatics who claim to speak for Islam; more recently by autocrats in foreign capitals who see free markets and open democracies and civil society itself as a threat to their power. The peril each poses to our democracy is more far-reaching than a car bomb or a missile. It represents the fear of change; the fear of people who look or speak or pray differently; a contempt for the rule of law that holds leaders accountable; an intolerance of dissent and free thought; a belief that the sword or the gun or the bomb or the propaganda machine is the ultimate arbiter of what's true and what's right.

Because of the extraordinary courage of our men and women in uniform, because of our intelligence officers, and law enforcement, and diplomats who support our troops—no foreign terrorist organization has successfully planned and executed an

"We all have to try harder. We all have to start with the premise that each of our fellow citizens loves this country just as much as we do; that they value hard work and family just like we do; that their children are just as curious and hopeful and worthy of love as our own."

attack on our homeland these past eight years. And although Boston and Orlando and San Bernardino and Fort Hood remind us of how dangerous radicalization can be, our law-enforcement agencies are more effective and vigilant than ever. We have taken out tens of thousands of terrorists—including bin Laden. The global coalition we're leading against ISIL has taken out their leaders and taken away about half their territory. ISIL will be destroyed, and no one who threatens America will ever be safe.

And to all who serve or have served, it has been the honor of my lifetime to be your commander in chief. And we all owe you a deep debt of gratitude.

But protecting our way of life—that's not just the job of our military. Democracy can buckle when it gives in to fear. So just as we, as citizens, must remain vigilant against external aggression, we must guard against a weakening of the values that make us who we are.

And that's why, for the past eight years, I've worked to put the fight against terrorism on a firmer legal footing. That's why we've ended torture, worked to close Gitmo, reformed our laws governing surveillance to protect privacy and civil liberties. That's why I reject discrimination against Muslim Americans, who are just as patriotic as we are. That's why we cannot withdraw from big global fights—to expand democracy, and human rights, and women's rights, and LGBT rights. No matter how imperfect our efforts, no matter how expedient ignoring such values may seem, that's part of defending America. For the fight against extremism and intolerance and sectarianism and chauvinism are of a piece with the fight against authoritarianism and nationalist aggression. If the scope of freedom and respect for the rule of law shrinks around the world, the likelihood of war within and between nations increases, and our own freedoms will eventually be threatened.

So let's be vigilant but not afraid. ISIL will try to kill innocent people. But they cannot defeat America unless we betray our Constitution and our principles in the fight. Rivals like Russia or China cannot match our influence around the world unless we give up what we stand for and turn ourselves into just another big country that bullies smaller neighbors.

Which brings me to my final point: our democracy is threatened whenever we take it for granted. All of us, regardless of party, should be throwing ourselves into the task of rebuilding our democratic institutions. When voting rates in America are some of the lowest among advanced democracies, we should be making it easier, not harder, to vote. When trust in our institutions is low, we should reduce the corrosive influence of money in our politics and insist on the principles of transparency and ethics in public service. When Congress is dysfunctional, we should draw our congressional districts to encourage politicians to cater to common sense and not rigid extremes.

But remember, none of this happens on its own. All of this depends on our participation; on each of us accepting the responsibility of citizenship, regardless of which way the pendulum of power happens to be swinging.

"Our Constitution is a remarkable, beautiful gift. But it's really just a piece of parchment. It has no power on its own. We, the people, give it power. We, the people, give it meaning. With our participation and with the choices that we make and the alliances that we forge."

Our Constitution is a remarkable, beautiful gift. But it's really just a piece of parchment. It has no power on its own. We, the people, give it power. We, the people, give it meaning. With our participation and with the choices that we make and the alliances that we forge. Whether or not we stand up for our freedoms. Whether or not we respect and enforce the rule of law. That's up to us. America is no fragile thing. But the gains of our long journey to freedom are not assured.

In his own farewell address, George Washington wrote that self-government is the underpinning of our safety, prosperity, and liberty, but "from different causes and from different quarters much pains will be taken . . . to weaken in your minds the conviction of this truth." And so we have to preserve this truth with "jealous anxiety"; that we should reject "the first dawning of every attempt to alienate any portion of our country from the rest or to enfeeble the sacred ties" that make us one.

America, we weaken those ties when we allow our political dialogue to become so corrosive that people of good character aren't even willing to enter into public service; so coarse with rancor that Americans with whom we disagree are seen not just as misguided but as malevolent. We weaken those ties when we define some of us as more American than others; when we write off the whole system as inevitably corrupt; and when we sit back and blame the leaders we elect without examining our own role in electing them.

PRESIDENT OBAMA sings "Amazing Grace" with church leaders while delivering a eulogy at the funeral of South Carolina state senator Clementa Pinckney, June 26, 2015, who was killed during the mass shooting on June 17 at the Emanuel African Methodist Episcopal Church in Charleston.

It falls to each of us to be those anxious, jealous guardians of our democracy; to embrace the joyous task we've been given; to continually try to improve this great nation of ours. Because for all our outward differences, we, in fact, all share the same proud title, the most important office in a democracy: citizen. Citizen.

So, you see, that's what our democracy demands. It needs you. Not just when there's an election, not just when your own narrow interest is at stake, but over the full span of a lifetime. If you're tired of arguing with strangers on the Internet, try talking with one of them in real life. If something needs fixing, then lace up your shoes and do some organizing. If you're disappointed by your elected officials, grab a clipboard, get some signatures, and run for office yourself. Show up. Dive in. Stay at it.

Sometimes you'll win. Sometimes you'll lose. Presuming a reservoir of goodness in other people, that can be a risk, and there will be times when the process will disappoint you. But for those of us fortunate enough to have been a part of this work and to see it up close, let me tell you, it can energize and inspire. And more often than not, your faith in America—and in Americans—will be confirmed.

Mine sure has been. Over the course of these eight years, I've seen the hopeful faces of young graduates and our newest military officers. I have mourned with grieving

THE OBAMAS watch the fireworks over the National Mall from the White House on July 4, 2009.

families searching for answers and found grace in a Charleston church. I've seen our scientists help a paralyzed man regain his sense of touch. I've seen wounded warriors who at points were given up for dead walk again. I've seen our doctors and volunteers rebuild after earthquakes and stop pandemics in their tracks. I've seen the youngest of children remind us through their actions and through their generosity of our obligations to care for refugees, or work for peace, and above all, to look out for each other.

So that faith that I placed all those years ago, not far from here, in the power of ordinary Americans to bring about change—that faith has been rewarded in ways I could not have possibly imagined. And I hope your faith has, too. Some of you here tonight or watching at home, you were there with us in 2004, in 2008, 2012—maybe you still can't believe we pulled this whole thing off. Let me tell you, you're not the only ones.

Michelle—Michelle LaVaughn Robinson, girl of the South Side— for the past 25 years, you have not only been my wife and mother of my children; you have been my best friend. You took on a role you didn't ask for, and you made it your own, with grace and with grit and with style and good humor. You made the White House a place that belongs to everybody. And the new generation sets its sights higher because it has you as a role model. So you have made me proud. And you have made the country proud.

Malia and Sasha—under the strangest of circumstances, you have become two amazing young women. You are smart and you are beautiful, but more importantly, you are kind and you are thoughtful and you are full of passion. You wore the burden of years in the spotlight so easily. Of all that I've done in my life, I am most proud to be your dad.

To Joe Biden—the scrappy kid from Scranton who became Delaware's favorite son—you were the first decision I made as a nominee, and it was the best. Not just because you have been a great vice president, but because in the bargain, I gained a brother. And we love you and Jill like family, and your friendship has been one of the great joys of our lives.

To my remarkable staff—for eight years—and for some of you, a whole lot more—I have drawn from your energy, and every day I tried to reflect back what you displayed—heart, and character, and idealism. I've watched you grow up, get married, have kids, start incredible new journeys of your own. Even when times got tough and frustrating, you never let Washington get the better of you. You guarded against cynicism. And the only thing that makes me prouder than all the good that we've done is the thought of all the amazing things that you're going to achieve from here.

And to all of you out there—every organizer who moved to an unfamiliar town, every kind family who welcomed them in, every volunteer who knocked on doors, every young person who cast a ballot for the first time, every American who lived and breathed the hard work of change—you are the best supporters and organizers anybody could ever hope for, and I will be forever grateful. Because you did change the world. You did.

"For all our outward differences, we, in fact, all share the same proud title, the most important office in a democracy: Citizen. Citizen."

"My fellow Americans, it has been the honor of my life to serve you. I won't stop. In fact, I will be right there with you, as a citizen, for all my remaining days."

And that's why I leave this stage tonight even more optimistic about this country than when we started. Because I know our work has not only helped so many Americans, it has inspired so many Americans—especially so many young people out there—to believe that you can make a difference—to hitch your wagon to something bigger than yourselves.

Let me tell you, this generation coming up—unselfish, altruistic, creative, patriotic—I've seen you in every corner of the country. You believe in a fair and just and inclusive America. You know that constant change has been America's hallmark; that it's not something to fear but something to embrace. You are willing to carry this hard work of democracy forward. You'll soon outnumber all of us, and I believe as a result the future is in good hands.

My fellow Americans, it has been the honor of my life to serve you. I won't stop. In fact, I will be right there with you, as a citizen, for all my remaining days. But for now, whether you are young or whether you're young at heart, I do have one final ask of you as your president—the same thing I asked when you took a chance on me eight years ago. I'm asking you to believe. Not in my ability to bring about change—but in yours.

I am asking you to hold fast to that faith written into our founding documents; that idea whispered by slaves and abolitionists; that spirit sung by immigrants and homesteaders and those who marched for justice; that creed reaffirmed by those who planted flags from foreign battlefields to the surface of the moon; a creed at the core of every American whose story is not yet written: yes, we can.

Yes, we did. Yes, we can.

Thank you. God bless you. May God continue to bless the United States of America. ★

FORMER PRESIDENT
BARACK Obama
waves with his wife
Michelle as they board
Special Air Mission
28000 at Joint Base
Andrews, Maryland,
January 20, 2017.

I dedicate this book to my donor, Yitzi Lemberger, aka "Spartacus."

—MARK GREENBERG

ACKNOWLEDGMENTS

ONE OF LIFE'S great pleasures is to say thank you to people. I agree with the saying "it is better to give than to receive." I know this firsthand as someone who owes his "second life" to another person.

First, to writer David Tait and designer Barbara Balch, who helped build this book page by page into the creation that it is: at the end of the day we always—well, usually—ended up on the same page, and they both worked tirelessly to make sure that what was made better could always be made better still. It was partly a shared admiration of our subject matter and then for each other.

A gigantic thank-you goes to Ken Burns for his wonderfully moving foreword and to his coordinating producer Elle Carrière—"behind every great man . . ."

My hat is off to the contributing voices in the book. First and foremost, to Rebecca Gitlitz, my lovely stepdaughter, and her delightful spouse, Samantha Rapoport. The joy you two exude together and share with all of us in this book is a tribute to the determination of this president and your love for each other. To Tweed Roosevelt, my "seems like" lifelong buddy from our two-month jungle adventure in Brazil—you are clearly your great-grandfather's great-grandson. Sir Richard Branson—28 years working and partying with you represents nearly 80 percent of my career. Thank you for sharing your thoughts on a man we both admire for making a difference for the planet, a subject I know is so important to you. And a debt of gratitude goes to the prolific photo impresario and author David Cohen, who sent me on my own to do this book. Also to Anastasia Somoza, daughter of my good friend and fellow photographer Gerardo Somoza: you are an extraordinary person. Gerardo, you and Mary have created greatness.

At Sterling Publishing, I am grateful to Barbara Berger, executive editor, for spearheading the project and deftly shepherding and editing the book; Chris Thompson, interior art director, for overseeing and guiding the beautiful design and intensive production process; Elizabeth Lindy, cover art director, for the stunning cover design; and to Kayla Overbey, proofreader extraordinaire.

To Seth Greenberg (no relation) and the legendary James Colton at ZUMA Press, who went the extra "smile" to be sure I had the best images possible from their exhaustive photo collection from news sources around the world. Thank you. Yes, *smile*. When will we next see a president whose photo should be in the dictionary under the words "joy" or "smile"? Rory Tait—everybody, remember this name. Rory, who was my first, and only, assistant, got the job done. He will either be an offensive tackle in the NFL or the commissioner one day—perhaps both! Thanks to Tammy Johnston at Embassy Row Pictures, who helped us display the "peak of Jerry Seinfield's existence" on these pages.

Thank you to Peter Riva, Michael Glavin, Joel Hecker, Gary Hairlson, the ever-brilliant Laurie Garrett, Samantha and Brian Tobe, Rhonda Weithman, Amy Wilhite, Charlotte Sheedy, and Professor Peter McQuown. To David Tait's buddy Bob Tewksbury—thanks for "pitching" in. You were all important players. My partner, Gail Zimmerman, deserves a medal of freedom for her steady disposition, patience, and continued love during the seven weeks this small team spent putting the book together.

Thank you, President Obama, for the example of your uncommon decency to a nation that so desperately needs it. Our better selves lurk within; we just need to find a way to channel them, just as we did on September 12, 2001, when we realized we are "all in it together." ★

—Mark Greenberg

NOTES

All speeches courtesy http://whitehouse.gov; other sources as follows:

16: The University of Virginia's Miller Center, http://bioguide.congress.gov, http://www.biography.com | 37: Wikipedia | 40: International Monetary Fund: https://www.imf.org/external/pubs, Standard and Poors | 52: Annenberg Foundation/factcheck.org | 53: Center for Automotive Research, J.D.Power |

92: www.slate.com, https://en.wikipedia.org | 100: https://history.state.gov/departmenthistory/travels/president/obama-barack | 104: http://www.businessinsider.com/features-of-air-force-one-2015-3 | 114: https://everytownresearch.org/gun-violence-by-the-numbers | 134,142,144: https://whitehouse.gov | 150: https://www.

theguardian.com, twittercounter.com/pages/100 | 161:www.whca.net | 167: http://www.newsweek.com/late-night-politicians-presidential-candidates-371394 | 172: https://www.washingtonpost.com/lifestyle | 176: https://en.wikipedia.org/wiki/Let›s_Move!

PHOTO CREDITS

Thank you to the extraordinary White House photo staff led by Pete Souza, and ZUMA Press, with their deep photographic resources.

Associated Press: © Laura Rauch: 12–13; **Courtesy of Sir Richard Branson:** 126; **Courtesy of Embassy Row Pictures:** 168 top and bottom; **Getty Images:** © Chuck Kennedy/AFP: 17; © Brooks Craft LLC/Corbis: 153; **Harvard Library:** 49; **Courtesy of C-Span:** 120–121,127, 163 center; **Courtesy of CBS:** 181 top; **Courtesy of NBC:** 82,199; markgreenbergphotography.com: 28–31, 34, 80, 82; **Courtesy of Patrick McQuown:** 156; **NASA:** Bill Ingalls: 142 top and inset, 143, 144 bottom right; **Marc PoKempner:** 10–11; **Courtesy of Bob Tewksbury:** 146; **Twitter/@Potus:** 158–159

The White House: Chuck Kennedy: 2, 76, 173 middle left, top left and right; Amanda Lucidon: 181 bottom right; Pete Souza: 4–6, 38–39, 46–47, 48, 50, 51 top left, 51 center, 51 bottom, 53–62, 90–91, 93–99, 100, 106, 110, 122–123, 151, 155 top right, 167 top left and right, 168, 170–171, 173 top left, 173 bottom left, 177, 179, 182–187, 188 all except top right, 189–190, 191 bottom; White House website: 198

ZUMA Press: © Drew Angerer/pool via CNP: 116–117, lower right; © Samantha Appleton: 180 bottom; © Karen Ballard: 24; © Carlos Barria/Reuters via Zuma Press: 107 top left; © Regina H. Boone/Detroit Free Press: 128; © Christy Bowe/Globe Photos: 144 (left column, 5th row), 178 bottom; © Pete Burbank/TNS via Zuma: 115; © Robert Cohen/St. Louis Post-Dispatch:

147; © Bao Danden/Xinhua: 180 top; © Al Diaz/TNS via Zuma Press: 99, 102–103 top left; © Olivier Douliery/CNP: 145, 157 top, 160–161, 163 bottom, 189 top; © Olivier Douliery/Pool/CNP, © Presa Internacional: 162 (left column, 3rd row); © Olivier Douilery/MCT via ZUMA: 18; © Larry Downing/Pool/CNP: 44–45; © Eboni L. Everson-Myart/Planet Pix: 136–137; © Jonathan Ernst: 192–193; © Jonathan Ernst/Reuters: 167 bottom; © Lisa Ferdinando/Planet Pix: 138 top; © Ryan Garza/Detroit Free Press: 128 top and bottom; © Yuri Gripas/Reuters: 162 (right column, 3rd row); © Handout Photos: 131; © Lawrence Jackson/Planet Pix: 66,127 bottom,148–149,179 center left; © Andy Katz/Pacific Press via Zuma Wire: 127 center left; © Chuck Kennedy/Planet Pix: 173 bottom right; © Kevin Lamarque/Reuters: 167 top, 144 (left column 4th row); © Chuck Liddy/MCT: 32, UPPA: 36; © Davi Lienemann/Planet Pix: 81; Amanda Lucidon: 178 top; © Jay Mallin: 77; © Pete Marovich/Pool/CNP: 162 (left column, 1st row); © Cheriss May/Nur Photo: 195, 144 (left column, 3rd row); © Brenden McDermid/Reuters: 205; © SSgt. Liliana Moreno/PlanetPix: 154 top; © Pete Marovich/pool: 164–165; © Rex Features: 51 top right, 132–133, 162 (right column, 2nd row), 166, 179 center right; © Rex Shuttersock: 162 (right column, 1st row); © Ron Sachs/CNP: 144 (right column, 3rd row); © Ron Sachs/Consolidated News Photos/Avalon:

144 (left column, 2nd row); © Damir Sagolj/Reuters via Zuma Press: 127 top; © Tami Silicio: 135; © Martin H. Simon/CNP: 162 (left column, 2nd row); © Pete Souza/Planet Pix: 41, 73, 75, 78, 84–85, 88, 102–103 top right, 104–105, 107 bottom right, 111 bottom, 112–113, 124, 125, 139, 140–141, 152, 154 bottom, 172, 173 middle, 174–175, 179 bottom right; © Chip Somodevilla/pool via CNP:108–109; © Pete Souza/The White House: 144 (left column, 1st row), 144 (right column, 1st row); © Sr/Rex Shutterstock, 144 (right column, 2nd row); © Abir Sultan/pool: 111 top right; © Timothy Tai: 130; © Patrick Tehan: 157 bottom; © Mike Theiler/Reuters: 191; © Shawn Thew/pool via CNP bottom left: 102, 155 bottom; © Kristoffer Tripplarr/pool/DPA: 163 top; © UPPA: 179 bottom left, 202; © Jeff Wheeler/Minneapolis Star Tribune: 188 top right; © Jim Young: 173 top; © Xinhua: 16, 22–23; © Yin Bogu/Xinhua/ZUMA Wire: 201

Newspapers: Courtesy of—*Bakersfield Californian*: 70; *Daily Star*: 86; *Denver Post*: 118; *Des Moines Register*: 70; *Hour*: 119; *Iowa City Press-Citizen*: 69; *Irish Times*: 21; *New York Daily News*: 71, 87; *Newsday*: 70; *el Nuevo Herald*: 86; *Orange County Register*: 118; *Longview News-Journal*: 119; *Post and Courier*: 119; *St. Louis Post-Dispatch*: 119; *Statesman Journal*: 118; *Taunton Daily Gazette*: 119; *Telegraph*: 86; *Virginia Pilot*: 71; Washington Times: 71

President Obama ✔
@POTUS44

🐦 Follow

I'm still asking you to believe - not in my ability to bring about change, but in yours. I believe in change because I believe in you.

9:13 AM - 20 Jan 2017

↩ 🔁 246,587 ♥ 495,208

THANK YOU PRESIDENT OBAMA